Heaven Tempers the Wind
Story of a War Child

Heaven Tempers the Wind: Story of a War Child

© Hazel Barker 2016

Published by Armour Books
P. O. Box 492, Corinda QLD 4075, Australia
www.armourbooks.com

Photo credits: Murmakova

ISBN: 9781925380057

National Library of Australia Cataloguing-in-Publication entry
Creator: Barker, Hazel M., 1937- author.
Title: Heaven tempers the wind : story of a war child / Hazel Barker.
ISBN: 9781925380057 (paperback)
Subjects: Barker, Hazel M., 1937---Childhood and youth.
World War, 1939-1945--Children--Burma--Biography.
World War, 1939-1945--Burma--Personal narratives.
Children and war--Burma.
Burma--History.

Dewey Number: 940.53092

No part of this book may be reproduced, stored in a retrieval system or transmitted in any form or by any means, without the prior permission in writing of the publisher, nor be otherwise circulated in any form of binding or cover other than that in which it is published and without a similar condition, including this condition, being imposed on the subsequent purchaser.

Heaven Tempers the Wind
Story of a War Child

Hazel Barker

Contents

Introduction		1
Chapter 1	The Party That Never Was	5
Chapter 2	On the Road to Mandalay	13
Chapter 3	Up the Irrawaddy to Katha	19
Chapter 4	Bombing of Katha	26
Chapter 5	The Refugee Camp	35
Chapter 6	My Family and Community	43
Chapter 7	School Days	56
Chapter 8	Summer Holidays	65
Chapter 9	More Holidays	74
Chapter 10	The Bamboo Telegraph	86
Chapter 11	Nightmare Trails and Terrible Tales	92
Chapter 12	Marooned by Monsoons	103
Chapter 13	Return to Katha	108
Chapter 14	Mandalay 1943	116
Chapter 15	Life in Mandalay	125
Chapter 16	Guerrilla Groups and Diverse Heroes	131
Chapter 17	Slavery, Sabotage and Germ Warfare	140
Chapter 18	Plague and Smallpox	149
Chapter 19	The Battle of the Box	160
Chapter 20	Hunger at the Farm	164
Chapter 21	Starvation, Beriberi and Malaria	176
Chapter 22	Return to Mandalay	186
Chapter 23	Victory	197
Chapter 24	A Period of Peace	203
Chapter 25	Sustained by Hope	211
Acknowledgments		220

This book is dedicated

*In loving memory
Of my mother,
May Josephine White,
Who peacefully passed away in Perth
On the eighteenth October, nineteen hundred and seventy six*

Introduction

Only two regular British battalions and four battalions of the Burma Rifles were stationed in Burma when Japan invaded the country. The two British battalions, the 1st battalion of the Gloucester regiment and the 2nd King's Own Yorkshire light infantry were used to maintain law and order, and were poorly equipped.

When the Japanese invaded Rangoon, the King's Own Yorkshire light infantry were sent into battle without steel helmets. No sniper rifles were issued to the KOYLIES, despite their high standard of shooting. Their 303 Vickers machine-guns were taken from the machine-gun platoon and handed over to a Burmese unit on aerodrome defence duties.

The guns were never used against the enemy.

Recruits had formerly been limited to the loyal hill tribes—Chins, Kachins and Karens—led by British officers. Later, due to political pressure, Burmese also were admitted into the Burma Rifles.

On the outbreak of war, these units proved disloyal to the British. They mutinied and murdered their British officers before joining the rebel Fifth Column. Anglo-Indian, Chin, Kachin and Karen units, on the other hand, remained loyal to their officers.

General Wavell, Supreme Allied Commander in South East Asia, underestimated the strength of the enemy, contemptuously referring to them as myopic, yellow men. In reality, the Japanese soldier was a formidable enemy. He believed that *harakiri*—death by suicide—was preferable to dishonour or disgrace.

Wavell appointed Lieutenant-General Hutton as Army Commander in Burma, and Major-General J.G. Smyth, VC, in command of the 17th Indian Division. Smyth arrived in Burma after the Japanese had taken Victoria Point on the southernmost tip of the country.

Soon after his arrival, the Burma Rifles were routed by the enemy from Tavoy. Cut off from the rest of Burma, the garrison south of Tavoy was compelled to escape by sea. Pursued to the docks, hand-to-hand fighting reminiscent of early pirating days ensued as they boarded the ships.

The retreat resulted in the loss of all airports south of Rangoon.

The Salween River, spawned in the mountains of China, forms part of the border between Burma and Thailand. Three kilometres wide, it forms the first natural line of defence. Between the Salween and the Irrawaddy Rivers, the short and swift Sittang River raises its club in defiance, pygmy-like, laying traps for its foes with dangerous and treacherous currents. Both the Salween and Sittang Rivers had fast-flowing currents, and protected Rangoon on its eastern side.

Only one solitary bridge spanned the Sittang River.

General Wavell expected Japanese forces to launch their major offensive on Rangoon via Thailand to the east. He passed orders to hold the Japanese forces at the Salween River. If they were unable to halt the enemy, they were to fall back and hold them at the Sittang.

The Salween failed to check the enemy. Weakened by malaria, the Allies were outnumbered three to one, with poor equipment and lack of air and artillery support. They fought desperately, using bayonets and kukris, but were driven back.

During the retreat to the Sittang, the tired and thirsty men were harassed by low-level bombing as they trudged through the hot, dusty terrain. After dark the enemy exploded tracers and firecrackers. Mules panicked and stampeded, carrying off the wireless sets.

The retreating army moved across the Sittang River under cover of night. Two thirds of the men were still on the other side when the Japanese attacked the next morning. On 23 February, informed that the combined road and railway bridge could not be held for more than an hour, Smyth gave orders to destroy it.

The men fought their way through dense jungle and Japanese lines, crossing the river on makeshift rafts. Others swam across after dumping their rifles in the river. Those who could not make it to the river surrendered. Five thousand men were killed, captured or missing in action.

For days after the destruction of the bridge, men continued to straggle back to their lines. The remnant was withdrawn to Pegu, re-armed and re-equipped with whatever was available.

After a respite of two days at Pegu, the town was heavily bombed. Intense fighting commenced. Road blocks were set up by the Burmese Fifth Column, but Allied troops broke through with the help of armoured tanks.

No troops were able to reach Rangoon in time to save her.

Chapter 1

The Party That Never Was

Rangoon 1941
My whole world changed on 23 December, the day of the Children's Christmas party. A lifetime has passed since then, but I recall each moment with vivid clarity. Mum rubbed the doorknobs with Brasso until they shone like gold. Cook took the Royal Doulton from the display cabinet in readiness for our roast dinner. My sister, June, and I helped Nanny shine the silver until the spoons reflected our faces.

I glanced at the large clock in the dining room. The Roman numerals were like so many matchsticks, but I could read the hours, the half-hours and the quarter-hours. The little hand had already passed nine. 'Should we dress for the party now, Mummy?'

'Not yet. Go into the garden with June. I'll tell you when it's time.'

Breathless, I rushed outside. Our front yard had a swing and seesaw. A coconut palm stood in the corner. The backyard held an outdoor gymnasium with Roman rings and parallel bars for my brothers. On the left were the servants' quarters, on the right a garage. In the centre, an almond tree provided us with shade and more nuts than we needed.

I listened for Mum to call us while we played on the seesaw. At ten years old, June was two years and six months older than I was. We were so close, yet so different—her skin the colour of milk chocolate and just as smooth. Her nose was neither aquiline like Dad's, nor as straight and shapely as Mum's, but in-between. I considered it quite cute. She was a born leader. Her buoyant spirit, thrilling stories and imaginative games ignited my love of adventure. She animated my colourless world like a rainbow. I followed her without question.

I had an olive complexion and soft dark brown hair. My short and stubby nose stuck like a blob of chewing gum in the centre of my face.

'Go in and check the time,' June said, after a while.

I raced indoors. It was just after half past ten. I rushed back, but before I could speak, the wail of sirens and the drone of aircraft filled the air. We gazed upwards. Each plane displayed a red sun on its wings.

Mrs Curry, our neighbour, had her fingers in her ears. She laughed as she walked backwards towards her bomb-shelter. Perhaps she thought it was a joke. None of us expected the war to reach us.

Without warning, bombs screamed from the sky.

At the first explosion, Dad ran to the air-raid shelter. He'd hired men to dig a deep L-shaped trench in the garden. It had a roof of metal sheets with a set of wooden steps at the entrance.

I knew a bomb could kill or maim us, but I wanted to save my dolls. I darted back to the house. From the corner of my eye, I saw Mum hand Baby Rose to Dad and fly after me. With a racing heart, I ran through the hallway, up the stairs to our playroom, and snatched Toddles. Unlike china dolls, my rag doll, Toddles, was tough.

Mum held out her arms as I tumbled back down the steps. We ran to the shelter through a choking cloud of dust. A burning smell spurred us on. Black clouds rose from the scorched earth to meet white puffs of smoke in the sky. Bombs thudded closer and closer.

Nanny had placed three cane chairs in the trench. Dad sat on one furthest from the entrance. Mum rushed to the chair next to him and bent over Baby, shielding her. I huddled at her feet. June had wedged herself between the two chairs. Nanny had put Herman on the floor beside her. He was already three but could neither walk nor talk.

Nanny covered her ears and cowered, down on her haunches. Dad's mother sat on the third chair. My other brothers, Rupert and Bertie, crouched closest to the opening.

Mum had showed us how to put our fingers in our ears during bombing. Still the explosions were deafening. My heart pounded so hard I thought it would burst. I took tiny disjointed breaths. The walls trembled. Grit and sand fell from the roof. We crouched, white and silent as ghosts, only letting out an occasional cough to clear our throats.

I read Mum's lips as they moved in silent repetitive prayer. 'Merciful Mother, have mercy on us.'

Grandmother, more voluble, kept muttering in a foreign language I didn't understand. Her voice grew louder and faster as the bombs whistled down. Her body rocked forwards and backwards as she prayed.

Unlike his mother, Dad remained silent. I had never seen him pray.

After the drone of the planes ceased, we still heard explosions and the roar of anti-aircraft guns in the distance.

As the 'All Clear' sounded, Rupert sprang to his feet and climbed out. 'Come on. Wonder what the city is like?'

A haze of dust hung in the air. Catching a whiff of smoke, we waved it from our faces. Mum and Dad crouched low and found their way out of the trench. I covered my mouth with one hand and, with the other, reached to June for comfort. We staggered out behind Mum.

Nanny didn't move.

Clouds of smoke rose, hiding the sun.

June returned to place her hand upon Nanny's shoulder. 'Come, Nanny, it's safe.'

Nanny's eyes were wide with fear. She shook her head, clasped her hands and pursed her lips.

June shrugged and went outside. She turned to me. 'What would you do if Mummy had been killed going back for you?'

The thought of losing my mother had never occurred to me. I couldn't imagine life without her. I remained silent.

My parents rushed towards the house. We were close behind as they entered the living room. Dad switched on our Phillips radio and slumped into his easy chair. His brows furrowed and his small eyes narrowed. Mum carried Rose to the settee. June and I sat either side of her to listen to the news. Rupert and Bertie occupied the two upright leather chairs.

The radio was on a corner table, covered with dust. The glass tulips on the centre table, as well as our lovely red carpet, were also dust-coated.

The newsreader cleared his throat. 'Do not listen to rumours. Here is the news. The city of Rangoon was bombed by wave after wave of aircraft. The bombing lasted for twenty minutes and there are many casualties.'

As Bertie began whispering to Rupert, Mum put a finger to her lips.

'The governor has ordered all schools to close and has advised everyone to evacuate further north and remain there until Britain has pushed back the invaders,' the newsreader concluded.

My parents sat in shocked silence. I was thrilled. I loved school, but I couldn't help smiling at the thought of having extra holidays.

Mum stood and smoothed her skirt. 'I'm going to the kitchen to look for Cook. He was preparing our meal when the bombing started.' On visibly shaky legs, she made her way to the kitchen, holding Rose. June and I followed. Dad and the two older boys remained in the living room. I didn't see Nanny. Perhaps she'd eventually left the trench and carried Herman to the landing overlooking the stairs. That was his usual spot—he would remain there during the day, on his own, giving no trouble except when he dirtied himself.

Mum's hands trembled as she opened the cooking pots. The rice had boiled dry and was ready for eating. The *dahl* bubbled away and the aroma of spices drifted to us. She switched off the stove. 'Cook must have fled during the bombing.'

She laid the table, placing a bottle of pickled cauliflower on it. 'The lentils and rice are cooked, but the meat isn't ready. We must be content with what we have.'

Questions flashed through my mind. Where had Cook gone? Was he lying dead somewhere? Why was no one searching for him? Glad our midday meal was ready, as we were going to the Christmas party after lunch, I glanced up at the clock on the wall. In my excitement, I found the Roman stick figures difficult to read. Surely it was time to dress for Santa?

'Mummy…'

She placed her finger to her lips and led June away.

I didn't follow. I raced upstairs to check whether Nanny had laid my party frock on the bed. The pink frilly dress was powdered with dust. The house had never been so dusty.

Why did Mum go off with June? What secret was she telling her? Then I knew. Santa must be dead. The bombs had killed him.

How would Christmas be without Santa? Who'd bring us our toys? I couldn't wait to hear the news. I sat on the banister and slid to the bottom of the stairs—the quickest way.

Mum and June met me in the hallway. 'The party's cancelled. We can't go,' June said.

'Is Santa dead? Is Rudolph hurt?'

Mum shook her head. 'No. They're all right, but it's not safe to be out. The Japanese planes may come back.'

'Oh, no. No. No.' A lump rose to my throat and tears welled in my eyes. I'd looked forward to the party for so long. I thought of the toys, balloons, bon-bons, cakes and sweets. June had told me Santa would give everyone a present from beneath a large Christmas tree.

She took my hand. 'We're going away for a holiday. We'll have a really cold Christmas. Maybe even snow. It'll be fun.'

Mum nodded. 'Let's go and pack.' She bit her lip.

Dad emerged from the living room. 'I'm going to take the boys with me to see what we can find out.' He stomped down the passage with Rupert and Bertie in tow. In seconds, the car engine grumbled to life and they drove off.

I clutched Toddles as I watched them leave. I longed to go with my brothers.

Rupert had an aquiline nose and swarthy skin like Dad's. Even at twelve, his shoulders were broader and his muscles far more developed than other boys his age. Strong and fearless, he protected Bertie from bullies at school.

Bertie was a year younger than Rupert. He had a cleft chin and Mum's cupid bow lips. I adored his charming smile and white, well-shaped teeth. He was wiry but not as brave as Rupert.

My thoughts were interrupted by June. 'Come, Hazel. Let's help Mum with the packing.'

I glanced at our swing and seesaw. No time to play now. I followed my sister up to our room and began to throw clothes into a suitcase. When June had finished packing her portmanteau, she helped me fold my clothes neatly so there was space for lots more.

***

When we heard the vehicle returning, we raced outside. Dad and the boys tromped into the house. Dad looked grim and forbidding. Rupert was breathing heavily and Bertie had a dazed look in his eyes. I dared not ask them what they'd seen, but crept upstairs.

The boys passed me on the way. They entered their room, slamming the door shut. I remained on the stairway, undecided and uneasy, until I heard my parents talking in the living room.

I slipped my shoes off and tiptoed towards their voices. 'Bombs landed on the docks, the markets, Strand Road, Phayre Street, Lewis Street, Judah Ezekiel Street and around the Shwe Dagon Pagoda and the aerodrome,' Dad said. 'Fires raged everywhere and the dead lay where they'd fallen. Coolies who would normally have carried away the corpses were themselves lying dead or wounded. Crows were feasting on the cadavers. The stench was terrible.'

'Why didn't the people run for shelter?' Mum asked.

'The natives obviously didn't realise the danger they were in even when the sirens sounded. Apparently they all stood and watched the planes fly in.'

Mum gave a half-gasp and a half-sob. I flew upstairs to give June the news. She listened, wide-eyed. Then we raced to the boys' room.

Rupert and Bertie were huddled together in deep conversation.

'What did you see?' June burst out.

Bertie shook his head, too emotional to speak.

Rupert didn't hesitate. 'We saw cows with their guts spilling out on the road.'

'The poor things!' I said.

They heard the sound of footsteps ascending the stairs, and waved us off.

Leaving their room, we met Dad and Mum in the corridor. The ash from the fire had given Dad's black hair a greyish look. 'I'll break the news to Granny and help her pack.' His voice sounded tired and his shoulders slumped.

Within an hour they got into the car and set off.

'Where's Daddy taking her?' I asked.

'To the station. She's going to join your aunt and cousins at a farm,' Mum answered.

Even before the bombing, our uncle, solicitous for his wife and children, had sent them to the countryside, not far from Mandalay. U Ka was a rector at Rangoon University. He'd married Dad's sister, Jhan.

'So Granny won't be living with us?'

'Not any more. Our home is getting too crowded and Aunty's house is bigger than ours.'

A few hours later, Dad returned. His brows were furrowed. Beads of sweat lay on his upper lip. 'We'll leave early tomorrow and take as much as we can.'

***

The next morning, I kissed all my dolls goodbye. I had no regrets. Our toys always remained at home during our vacation. I gave Toddles an extra hug. Thrilled at the prospect of a holiday, my only concern was that Santa would be unable to deliver our presents. Although I had sixteen dolls, I'd written asking him for another.

I left my bedroom with its pink curtains and little white cot, then went to the toilet. The fresh odour of phenol followed me as I ran downstairs to the car for the long journey north.

Mum sat in front with Baby on her lap. Rupert and Bertie carried our trunks and suitcases to our car, soon filled to capacity with three adults and six children. I glanced back at the whitewashed two-storey quarters and waved goodbye to luxury, piped water, showers and baths, unaware of what lay ahead.

Dad must have avoided the bombed areas. We saw no damage but we smelled the lingering smoke. Grey clouds covered the sky even though it was the cold, dry season. Dad remained silent as he drove, but the two boys chatted endlessly. I strained my ears and caught fragments of conversation.

'Hundreds died,' Rupert said. 'Most of them were Indians and Burmese.'

After a brief silence, Bertie added, 'Japs hit every building in the airport, even the control tower.'

'But the Royal Air Force and the American Volunteer Group shot down thirteen enemy planes.'

'Lucky they missed the telegraph office or the Anglo-Indian telephonists who kept working would've been killed.'

Their voices were lost in the increasing roar of traffic. We passed trucks heading for Rangoon to pick up the military supplies America had shipped. All the drivers were Chinese. They beeped their horns and swore at the traffic ahead. Bullock carts choked the sides of the highway, kicking up clouds of dust. The roads had never been so crowded when we had driven to the hills for our holidays before.

Mum wound up the car window. 'Lucky it's winter or we'd die with the heat.'

Squeezed between Mum and Dad, I gazed at the trucks with their canvas roofs flapping in the wind. Years later, I learned many of them careered off cliffs on their way to China.

Chapter 2

On the Road to Mandalay

Blissfully ignorant of the danger surrounding us, I was still aware of a sense of urgency. Dad intended to drive as far as Mandalay, in the centre of Burma. From there, he hoped to take a steamer upriver to Katha. The provincial town was situated on a plain hemmed in between mountains and the Irrawaddy River. Britain had set up a refugee camp for their employees in a village not far from Katha, almost three hundred kilometres north of Mandalay.

Dad concentrated on the traffic. The countryside was dotted with termite hills, some as high as houses. A patchwork of paddy fields gave way to teak trees, then sparse forests. Cattle grazed on meagre pasture further inland, as we headed towards the dry belt.

About halfway to Mandalay, Dad pulled in at a bungalow reserved for government employees. It was getting dark and the cottage looked warm and inviting.

Even before we got out of the car, the caretaker ran towards us. 'Sorry, Mr White, Sir, but it's already occupied. Everyone is heading north, and another official checked in last night.' He knew my father because Dad had often stopped there while accompanying a judge on tour of the country courts.

'You can't drive the whole night. You must rest somewhere.' Mum looked worn out from cradling six-month-old Rose, and Dad smelled of sweat. We all needed a shower.

Dad scratched his head. 'We could sleep at a *zayat*.'

What on earth was a *zayat*? It sounded like a zoo.

'What's a *zayat*?' Mum asked, as if in answer to my thoughts. She wasn't fluent in Burmese.

'A rest house where travellers shelter.' A few minutes later, Dad pulled up at a raised wooden platform with a thatched roof. We all got out of the car and stretched.

Mum screwed up her face. 'I'll sleep in the car. A leper may have slept there.'

I climbed onto the platform and looked around. It stood off the road in a clearing, surrounded by jungle. Would a tiger spring out of the bushes and attack us as we slept?

Nanny laid down a canvas ground sheet for herself and Herman, my crippled brother, then stretched out for a good night's sleep. I watched her with envy. But I didn't want to catch leprosy or be eaten by a tiger, so I curled up in the back of the car with June and the boys. My parents slept upright in the front with Rose between them. Worn out with the long drive, I slept peacefully in spite of the overcrowding.

***

The sun hadn't risen when Mum woke us on Christmas morning. My foot had been tucked under June and was asleep. Rupert's hair stood up like a shaving brush. Mum's looked neat and tidy, so I combed mine with my hands before getting out of the car. She shivered, her arms crossed. I circled my arms around myself too and rubbed the goose pimples on them.

Mum wished everyone a 'Happy Christmas' and kissed us. Tears glistened in her eyes.

I ran and wished everyone a merry Christmas. They returned my greetings, but no one sounded cheerful. Perhaps they, too, missed their toys.

Always so full of fun, Bertie smiled. But his eyes didn't sparkle as they usually did.

Mum disappeared into the jungle for a few minutes.

'Be careful of snakes,' she said as June and I dashed off into the bushes to relieve ourselves. Dad and the boys went off in another direction.

Nanny cleaned Herman, who had soiled himself as usual. He'd remained as helpless as a baby ever since he'd been born. The rest of us washed our faces with water from a well and climbed into the car. Mum bit her beautiful cupid bow lip into a thin line. Shoulders slumped, Dad set the heavily laden car in motion, and we soon re-joined the traffic heading north.

Dad drove on until we came to a roadside stall near a town. Stopping for breakfast, he bought a newspaper and ordered toast and eggs for each of us. Nanny fed Herman with some rice gruel and ate a bowl of fried rice.

Dad shook out the paper and read the news. 'The exodus from Rangoon continues. Refugees stream northwards. They squeeze into any available space on trains, hang outside carriages, or sit on the roof.' He gulped his coffee. 'Better leave as soon as we can.'

Mum turned to us. 'Go to the toilet.'

I rose from my seat at the wooden table to join June in the long queue for the public toilets. Some people had wandered off into the jungle nearby, but I waited rather than risk being seen with my panties down.

We crammed back into our car and moved on. Why was everyone so silent?

***

We finally arrived in Mandalay, late in the afternoon on Christmas Day. I saw no signs of the festive season. I'd been hoping to catch the sights in the city centre. This was the city of my birth, after all. But Dad drove straight to the waterfront. He intended to go as far as Katha by boat as quickly as possible. Hawkers were everywhere, shouting and selling their wares. Food stalls lined both sides of the road. The river was crowded with river barges, fishing boats and launches belonging to the Irrawaddy Flotilla Company. It was so muddy and broad I couldn't see the opposite bank. The place smelled of stale fish and the natives stank of sweat.

We didn't know then that, during our journey, messages had been flying back and forth between the Prime Ministers of England and Australia. Churchill requested Curtain to send an Australian division to defend Rangoon. Curtin refused.

***

Christmas 1941 was so unlike other Christmases. No parcels to open, no toys to play with, no Christmas cheer.

The previous December, Mum had put me to bed earlier than usual because Santa was to visit at midnight. I had lain awake, hoping to greet him, but soon fell asleep. Early next morning, June woke me. A lovely rag doll, Toddles, peeped out from a lucky stocking filled with all sorts of treasure. Parcels of various shapes and sizes lay at the foot of my bed.

June had received a shut-eye china-doll with leather shoes.

After we'd opened our presents, we raced downstairs to show them to the family. A Christmas tree stood in our lounge room with more toys. Streamers and balloons hung from the ceiling. Rupert sat on the carpet, devouring a copy of *Boys Own Annual*. Bertie sprawled on the carpet with a meccano set. He'd already built himself a bridge.

Happy among mounds of coloured wrapping paper and cocoons of ribbon, we played with our new toys until breakfast. Herman was only two years old then; he was still asleep in his cot. Rose hadn't been born.

Oranges, walnuts, sweets and a Christmas cake with the words, *Merry Xmas* in white icing, lay invitingly on the table. We helped ourselves to anything we wanted, and waited for Mum to cut the cake. For dinner, we had roast goose, followed by plum pudding and mince pies. Then it was time for pulling crackers, for whistles and balloons, paper hats, funny masks and reading out mottoes and riddles.

The day had ended at the cinema with *The Christmas Carol*.

***

Now, at Mandalay's riverside docks, there was no Christmas cheer.

Hundreds of Chinese milled around.

'Why are so many Chinese here?' June asked.

'They're hoping to escape into Yunnan,' Mum replied.

I turned to June. 'Where's Yunnan?'

Mum shifted Rose and glanced down at me. 'In China. They're trying to return to their homeland. This is the only way out for them. China is already in the throes of war but they'd rather go home and risk death than die in a foreign land.'

Dad opened the bonnet and fiddled with the engine.

I heard the sound of hammering. 'What's Daddy doing?'

'He's disabling the vehicle so the Japanese can't use it.'

Tilting my head to one side, I pursed my lips. My mind raced, searching for answers.

'The government passed an order to immobilise all privately owned automobiles,' Rupert said. 'Our Chevrolet is now as useless as a perforated purse.'

My chest tightened. 'Will someone take care of our car?'

Mum nodded, but her eyes turned to a burned sedan not far off. My mind went back to the time we had driven to Kalaw for a holiday and our old Austin had caught fire straining up a steep hill.

Dad shut the bonnet of the car, flung the hammer down, and strode towards the ticket office. A sign informed us no cabins were available, so Dad sent Bertie ahead to lay a blanket on deck and mark our spot. Slowly, the long line of people in the queue moved forward.

We finally succeeded in getting tickets and pushed our way to Bertie. He stood, surrounded by half a dozen shouting Chinese, bristling like a terrier fending off a herd of bulls. The pain in my chest grew worse. Were they going to bash Bertie up?

Dad gripped his double-barrelled gun and strode up to Bertie. The men backed off. Dad's brows creased in a frown. 'The place is filthy. Find something to sweep our area.'

Bertie slunk off. When he returned, he held a broom and slid it on the floor towards the rails.

'Don't you even know how to handle a broom? Do you wish people to think you're a rich man's son?' Dad yelled.

Mum's face crumpled. 'Of course Bertie can't sweep. The Indian sweeper has always swept our floors.'

My heart went out to Bertie. Dad had humiliated him in front of strangers. I wanted to tell Bertie how brave he'd been, but I didn't dare. I stood welded to the spot, staring at my brother, wishing I could help.

Dad glared at us. 'Sit down unless you want to lose our place.'

I sat near the rails and dangled my feet below. Gritting my teeth, I swiped at my tears, trying to hide them. This wasn't like other holidays.

'You'll get wet from the waves once the steamer starts to move.' Mum feared drowning and told us to pray that Japanese bombers wouldn't follow us.

At the time, we didn't know we were safe for a while as enemy planes were busy bombing Allied troops at Rangoon and the surrounding area.

But even in northern Burma, we would not escape further raids.

Chapter 3

Up the Irrawaddy to Katha

I only have a hazy recollection of the three hundred kilometre trip up the Irrawaddy. Mum placed Baby on the blanket beside her but found it difficult to sit on the floor. The boat was crowded. Dad wouldn't allow us to wander about. When we went to the toilet, he told Rupert and Bertie to accompany us and wait outside. He said he didn't trust the Chinese, who spoke loudly and appeared to be quarrelling.

Mum took out a tin of Huntley and Palmer's biscuits and gave one to Rose. Before boarding, Mum had filled our tiffin carrier—a stack of round metal containers—with enough to last our journey, normally about twenty hours.

Nanny served us on the enamel plates she'd brought along. We scooped up the food with our spoons, as if we were at a picnic.

I folded my arms and stretched my legs, crossing and re-crossing them all the time. I couldn't see the river from our position on deck. Worst of all, Herman soiled his pants. I was so embarrassed. Our area stank like a public toilet that had never been cleaned.

***

The steamer stopped to take on more people. I wondered how they would all fit, but they managed to squeeze in. A newspaper vendor also came on board. Passengers rushed forward and he soon sold the lot. Fortunately, Dad was able to buy one.

He settled down with a cup of coffee Mum had poured for him and opened the newspaper. 'Bombers attacked Rangoon again on Christmas day. A bomb exploded on the Strand Hotel, but they're remaining open. Six hundred died and thousands have left the city.'

He took a few sips of coffee before continuing. 'Police and clerical staff desert in droves. *Dacoits*—armed robbers—loot houses and shops. Rangoon remains without water or electricity. Corpses lie rotting on streets. Civil administration has crumbled.' He set aside the paper and shoved his way towards the toilets.

Rupert snatched the newspaper. 'The General Hospital is filled with civilian casualties. Most of the staff left for Mandalay on a special train with wounded soldiers abroad. Hundreds, who had been incarcerated in prisons and asylums, now run freely in the city. Inmates of the leper asylum squat on the roadside. Reptiles and wild animals, released from the zoo by an over-anxious animal-loving official, wander on the roads, adding to the chaos.'

I imagined stray dogs licking the lepers' open sores, tigers prowling the streets and lions dragging people off into the bushes. I shuddered.

***

We arrived at Katha about noon on Boxing Day. Dad hired two pony carts and the boys loaded them up, then squeezed in among the cases. The rest of us got into the other. As we drove off, I looked back at the huge muddy river where sampans bobbed up and down. The boatmen had painted eyes on their sharp beak-like bows and they looked like vultures.

As the ponies clomped along, we saw the market and, beyond it, a large concrete wall about six metres high.

'That's the jail,' Mum said.

We passed a crumpled pagoda and several banyan and flame-of-the-forest trees. The red flowers were, it seemed, prophetic of the tongues of fire later to engulf the small town.

Dad hoped to be back at Rangoon within six months. He didn't want to hide in the refugee camp, where the High Court staff and their families had evacuated. So he found lodgings at a house built on stilts and nestled in a beautiful rose garden. I was so glad he had rented in the suburbs as most houses were small and close together with no gardens.

I'd get up early, grab a pair of scissors and pick the roses before anyone else awoke. I sniffed each flower and inhaled its fragrance before placing it in a basket. The fresh morning breeze played around my face as the birds sang an unfamiliar melody. I licked my lips, thinking of the tomato juice Nanny made for breakfast. Since Cook had disappeared, Nanny prepared our meals and looked after Herman while Mum took charge of Rose.

After some fresh fruit and cereal, June played with me in the garden. The tightness in my chest disappeared and tingling warmth spread throughout my body.

I was unaware that, less than a hundred and sixty kilometres north of us, Allied aircraft were airlifting the wounded from Myitkyina over to India. Refugees had taken the train all the way to the railway terminus there, hoping to fly out.

***

The first wave of evacuees took the train from Rangoon to Prome, then trekked westwards over the Arakan hills to Akyab, the closest seaport to India. From there, they boarded a motor launch to Chittagong in India.

As the Japanese advanced into Burma, the next wave of refugees moved to Monywa, a town about ninety kilometres due west of Mandalay. They then trudged northwards via the Kawbaw Valley.

Years later, I came to know Lieutenant Colonel Derek Bartells who related the tragic incidents he had witnessed during the trek. 'One morning, we saw a man crossing a roaring river with a boy on his shoulders and a woman clinging to his waist. He'd already done two trips and was exhausted by then, but gave it a go anyway. Seeing the load was too much for him, the woman released her hold and was swept off by the current.'

'Did she survive?' I asked.

'No. He'd reached the middle of the river when she let go. I think his wife realised she was placing an impossible burden on him and chose to sacrifice her life for the family.'

***

We were safely ensconced at Katha during early 1942 while evacuees were trekking over the mountains into India. How well I remember those days. Mum took us aside and told us that, if we ever had to leave in a hurry, we had to fill a Shan bag with our clothes. 'I'll be busy packing milk and food for Baby and the rest of us, and won't be able to help you pack,' she warned.

Dad took us to find shoes suitable for hiking. I squealed with delight at the thought of trekking across the mountains, as I loved walking in the hills at Kalaw during our summer holidays. The bazaar had low, palm-thatched stalls. People shouted and jostled each other, their various languages mingling. I saw many people of the hill tribes, especially Kachins.

As we gazed at the wares on offer, I sucked in my breath. French perfumes, fur wraps, high-heeled shoes and evening gowns were for sale in the black market. Many people who had already left had discarded their luxury items by the roadside and the locals had collected them to sell.

We found nothing suitable. 'The trekkers must have worn their most comfortable pair.' Dad bought tins of food and a couple of grey woollen army blankets. He even bought a hammock. When we returned, he strung it up between two jacaranda trees for us.

June kicked the ground and we launched ourselves into the air. 'Let's be fairies flying in the breeze,' she said.

We spent hours swinging in the sunshine until June left to help Mum with the baby. I let my imagination roam as I swung in the hammock. At Rangoon, we had a swing as well as a see-saw, but this hammock made up for their loss. Life was total bliss.

***

Singapore fell in February, and Rangoon was open to attack on all sides.

Churchill appealed for reinforcements, but the Australian Prime Minister Curtin refused permission for the diversion of an Australian troopship to Rangoon. He ordered the ship back to protect Australia's shores.

Unknowing, the Commanding Officer of the Gloucestershire Regiment in Rangoon prepared to receive the Australians at the docks.

Military engineers restored power to the electricity station and repaired the sewerage works. Soldiers patrolled the streets, shooting looters. The Chinese continued to transport American Lend-Lease stores along the Burma Road to Chungking.

Despite their efforts, large quantities were left behind. Rather than destroy them, British officers armed their men with guns and ammunition from stockpiles of abandoned equipment.

On 20 February, unable to defend the city without reinforcements, the Military Governor ordered civilians to evacuate. The last ship of British evacuees left Rangoon, too crowded to carry any more passengers.

Burmese thugs attacked those left behind, using half-metre long knives known as *dahs*. In a frenzy of fury, fed by Burmese nationalists who demanded independence from Britain, they hacked the evacuees. *Dahs* sliced through flesh and bone. Blood sprayed on onlookers and killers alike, leaving the street strewn with bodies.

Not far from Rangoon, villagers on a highway took advantage of the situation. They ambushed solitary cars carrying British and Indian refugees. They beheaded the males, then raped and killed the women.

We were fortunate to have left Rangoon before the massacres commenced. Reports of the carnage in that land of Buddhist belief and peaceful pagodas filtered through to my parents. They must have shared the news with Rupert, Bertie and June as I recall them being unusually quiet. Looking back now, I see the hand of God at work. We had been saved from certain death.

Rupert and Bertie went downtown daily. Each time they saw something new—hill tribes in their colourful clothes with silver ornaments, Chinese soldiers and civilians, hundreds of refugees. After scouring the town, they would explore the jungle, listening to the shrill of cicadas, the distant roar of tigers and the incessant chatter of monkeys. They would tell us of their exploits on their return.

Every evening after dinner, Nanny took Baby, June and me for a stroll in the large garden after she had tucked Herman into bed. Mum, Dad and the two boys listened to the news over the radio. Rupert was thirteen and Bertie twelve. When they joined us in the garden, they would be swearing vengeance on the Fifth Column for leading the Japanese through jungle paths and for placing blockades on roads. Dad ordered them to keep the truth from us, but Bertie told us of traitors, arsonists and looters, while keeping back the more gruesome details.

***

One evening, as the cold wind from the Himalayas made goose pimples rise on my arms, I went upstairs to fetch a cardigan. The place was in darkness, adhering to the blackout.

Dad was lounging in an easy chair with a glass of beer. As I eased forward, a figure darted across the room behind him. My brothers were downstairs, June was with Mum and Nanny with Herman. Baby slept in her cot.

Speechless, I bolted down the stairs to Mum. 'There's a man upstairs!'

Mum raced up the stairway and warned Dad.

'Why didn't she tell me? I could've had my head chopped off by the intruder. She's to search each room for him. Don't turn on the lights.'

Petrified, my heart pounded in my throat. I clutched Mum's hand. She summoned Rupert and Bertie. 'Bring a weapon with you.'

'Don't worry, Hazel,' June sang out. 'We'll find him if he's still here. Daddy's got a gun.' She stood beside Dad, his arm around her.

Armed with a stick each, the boys searched every room. Mum held my hand and followed them. I peered into the gloom, waiting for the man to slash out at us with his *dah*.

Dad remained where he was and drank his beer.

***

The next morning after breakfast, the boys left to explore the town. 'Hazel was terrified last night,' Mum said. 'I felt her trembling.'

Dad shrugged. 'She should have warned me straight away and not run off to you.' He glared at me and walked off.

Mum drew me to her. 'Your dad works for the British, and Burmese nationalists consider him an enemy. You *know* that they kill everyone who is a friend of Britain. He wants you to go to him in future and not run to me.

He *knew* the intruder had already fled, but he meant to teach you a lesson.'

Would the man have hacked my father's head off, or did he creep upstairs to steal something, and I'd surprised him?

Despite that scare, I still thought we were on holidays. I soon forgot the incident and continued to get up early each morning to pick roses.

Chapter 4

Bombing of Katha

A slight breeze arose, carrying the perfume of roses with it. The cool weather invigorated me as I swung in the hammock. We had been at Katha four months.

Further south, after the fall of Rangoon in March 1942, the Allies had regrouped in central Burma. Drenched in perspiration, the troops trudged northwards towards the oilfields on the highway flanking the Irrawaddy River. The odour of gunpowder and petrol assailed their nostrils and stung their eyes. Gunfire and bombs blasted their ears.

Casualties travelled to Mandalay by river and rail, their wounds re-opening from the constant jolting. Where rot had already set in, bandages oozed with pus. Flies settled on the dressings.

The First Burma Division under Major General Bruce Scott took up defensive positions at Yenangaung to protect the oil fields. When Japanese troops advanced to within a few kilometres of the town, British engineers destroyed the petroleum, the generators and power station.

Amid clouds of black and orange smoke, the enemy infiltrated their position, captured the entire source of water and blocked their only line of retreat. Heat from the fires increased the temperature to 51 degrees Celsius. Men cried out through parched lips with nothing to quench their thirst. They fought on, praying for help, as they held the Japanese back for two days.

Death seemed inevitable. But God answered their prayers. The Chinese 38th Division under General Sun cut through the Japanese blockade and rescued them.

In less than a month, however, Japanese ships brought in fresh forces from Singapore and recaptured Yenangaung.

***

I was still in my idyll of ignorance. One day Bertie blurted out, 'Rangoon has been burned and Scott Market razed to the ground. Charred bodies are everywhere. Vultures and crows are feasting on them.'

I slumped in my seat and covered my face. Scott Market! I pictured the shops before Christmas—the toys displayed in shop windows and the shops containing bolts of material. After Rowe & Company and Whiteaways, the shopping plaza was my favourite place for toys. I trembled at the terrible tragedy.

***

One day we were in the Market Square when people gathered to question a young man, just arrived from Rangoon. The crowd clamoured for information. Even stall-holders left their wares unattended. I hid behind Bertie.

'Shops in Rangoon's commercial centre are barred and shuttered. Burmese are hacking Indians to death with *dahs*. We drove past Indians who trudged northwards in groups of thirty to fifty,' the man said.

'With *dacoits* about, they couldn't take any chances.' Dad spoke *sotto voice*, to no one in particular.

The stranger stopped to sip from his water bottle. 'They moved like animals in a pack. The women and children were surrounded by men and boys armed with clubs.'

Someone from the crowd shouted, 'Did they walk all the way from Rangoon to Mandalay? That's a four hundred-mile journey.'

The man continued speaking, as if there'd been no interruption. 'Some tried to carry so much—they had to discard things on the way.'

'Yes. When we left, people got rid of excess baggage like gramophone records by the roadside.' Dad's voice was a bit louder. 'We left most of our possessions behind. Thugs have probably ransacked our home by now.'

My thoughts wandered to Rangoon. *Had thieves ransacked our house?*

Had they taken our HMV gramophone? Mum had showed me the picture of a dog listening to his master's voice and taught me to appreciate music. Bertie used to sing along with operatic arias. He'd write down the words and replay the record until he got down every word.

My musical tastes later turned classical but, as a child, I enjoyed the latest pop songs like *Ferry Boat Serenade* and *Roll out the Barrel*.

With a sudden jolt, I returned to the present when Dad put a hand on the man's shoulder as he was about to leave. 'Did they make it to Mandalay?'

'Some died on the way.' The man threw out his arms. 'They were a bedraggled lot, especially the females. Blood streamed from their noses and ears.'

Dad raised his brows.

'You *know* how Indian women wear solid gold nose and ear rings. The *dacoits* wrenched them off.' The man gazed around him. 'God help us if the Japs get this far … and it looks like they will.' He lapsed into silence.

His actions portrayed the desperation and the futility of it all. Even *I* felt some impending doom hanging over us.

***

My parents must have been aware of the rapid advance of Japanese troops. Not long after I'd seen the intruder, we hired two pony carts and moved to the town centre. 'Why are we leaving, Mummy?' I choked back tears and compressed my lips.

'Remember when you saw that man in the house? Well, it's no longer safe to live in the suburbs. We're too isolated here.'

On our way to the town, we passed a church and several white bungalows where Europeans lived. Phlox, larkspur, hollyhock and petunias grew in their gardens, and I longed for the Rangoon University gardens where we used to play with our cousins.

Our new brick home stood close by others on the street. Mum looked up at the metal sheet roof. 'It will be noisy when the monsoons start and the rain pelts down.'

We did not stay long enough to find out.

The week after we moved, Japanese planes droned over and discharged their bombs. The ground vibrated and fires blazed all around. Unlike Rangoon, no sirens warned us. No anti-aircraft guns fired at the enemy. Nor did we have a trench to shelter in. June and I ran to Mum and huddled close.

My brothers were out.

'Where are the boys?' Mum bit her lip and hugged Baby.

We waited for them to turn up. Dad paced up and down the living room.

Mum pursed her lips and glanced at Rose. A long shuddering sigh escaped her. 'Your father should've sent us by plane to India when we still had the chance. I was too afraid to suggest anything.'

She glanced at our accumulated stacks of tinned provisions and stocks of food. 'If only we'd gone to the refugee camp with the others, we wouldn't have to abandon everything now.'

The thought of losing all my frocks and shoes made me cringe.

A few minutes later, Rupert and Bertie dashed in. Their clothes were dusty and covered with patches of black. Rupert didn't pause to talk, but raced into his room. I heard him rummaging around.

Bertie came to us, his face flushed. 'The bombs rained down, and we flung ourselves on the ground. I lay face down. Rupert threw himself on his back and watched the missiles whistling down.'

Bertie's story held me entranced. I searched for signs of blood. 'Were you hit?'

He shook his head. 'The blast of the explosion spewed up tons of dust and mortar. Our eyes stung and our ears buzzed. After the bombing, Rupert sat up and moved his jaws sideways before getting up. His ears must have felt queer, like mine did. We sped up the street. It was strewn with rubble, and the buildings were no longer there. A wall remained standing in a heap of ruins. People were making their way to the bank vaults. We squeezed past. Dust-covered bank notes and gold sovereigns were scattered all over. Several yards off, the steel doors lay, twisted and torn.'

'Did you bring back anything?' I interrupted.

Bertie ignored me. 'Rupert blinked. His eyes were red from the dust. He told me to race home and get something to put the money in, then made his way over the rubble, collected coins, and shoved them into his pockets. I crawled forward. A man with clothes still smouldering picked up some cash and left.'

Bertie delved into his pocket. A cloud of dust arose as he fumbled for something.

Rupert dashed out of his room with a knapsack on his back.

Dad placed a restraining hand on his shoulder. 'Where are you going?'

'To gather gold.'

Dad's voice rose. 'From where?'

Rupert shuffled his feet, obviously eager to leave. 'The bank. The safe is wide open. There are stacks of cash lying around.'

'May I come too?' *I'd buy so many dolls with that money.*

Mum dragged me aside. 'In times like this it's best for us to be together. You never know what people will do for just a few coins.'

'Watch out for thugs…' Dad began.

Rupert cut him off. 'Gold is lying around waiting to be gathered. Everyone is collecting the stuff.' He turned to leave.

I conjured up visions of shining sovereigns cascading out of a safe and into the Rupert's knapsack.

Dad must have pictured something very different. My brothers were already at the door when he grabbed Rupert's arm. His voice rose to a crescendo. 'No. Remain here with your mother.'

Rupert slunk back to his room. I heard him fling his knapsack onto the wooden floorboards. I guess he visualised the books he could have purchased to fill his library.

A few minutes later, a low flying plane and the stutter of machine guns shattered the silence.

'Jap planes are strafing the crowds at the bank vaults.' Dad looked out of the window and watched the planes as they dived.

Bombs descended. Billowing towers of smoke symbolised the black despair that overcame us. Houses ignited, sending balls of burning flame into the air like a million firecrackers. Infernos raged through the town.

'Hurry before the whole block catches fire.' Dad herded us into the street.

This time, I didn't turn back to retrieve anything. My dolls were still in Rangoon.

We stood on the pavement outside the house. Smoke drifted towards us, carrying the smell of gunpowder. Flames crackled, accompanied by an occasional explosion. People fled, shouting warnings that the Japanese army was close.

After some time, we heard the planes departing. They left us in comparative silence. Only the crackling of flames or the boom of a petrol or ammunition dump exploding disturbed the quiet. Crowds milled around, talking and gesticulating—preparing to trek over the hills into India. A woman balanced a bundle containing food and clothing on her head. Another bounced along with a yoke over her shoulder. One basket held all her possessions, the other a baby.

A man beckoned to an Indian, then handed him some notes. The coolie placed the man's pile of goods in two baskets slung on either end of a bamboo yoke.

'Join our group. There'll be strength in numbers,' someone called to Dad.

He shook his head. 'I've six kids. I can't think of such a gruelling trek.' He turned to Mum. 'Take the older children and try to escape. I'll remain with the others. Nanny will look after us.'

Mum wrung her hands in despair. 'We can't break up the family. We must stay together and trust in God's mercy.'

I gaped at her. I'd have been happy to take my chance with her, but wondered if Dad had included me among the younger ones. I couldn't imagine him parting from June. *Perhaps he meant that June, Herman, Baby and I were to remain behind.* I went over to Mum and held her hand.

My father was always so strict and had never allowed Mum to go anywhere on her own. *Had he really meant to let her trek to India without him?* At the time, I could not understand my father's words and, over the years, I've often pondered what he'd said.

Had he chosen to relinquish his fair-complexioned Anglo-Indian wife who would draw the attention of Japanese militia and get us all interned in concentration camps? Hoped to gain the sympathy of his wealthy relatives for his young children?

The refugees moved off, hoping to reach India before the monsoons commenced.

We were alone in a deserted street. The town was oddly silent, despite the crackle of flames and gusts of wind.

Dad stood stupefied. He looked unable to decide whether to go or stay.

A jeep-load of British soldiers drove up. The officer-in-charge sported a clipped moustache. 'Leave the town immediately. Churchill has declared a scorched earth policy and everything is to be destroyed.'

'But we have no transport,' Dad said.

'Take what you can and get out. Don't delay.' The officer gave a brief nod to the driver, who stepped on the accelerator.

The vehicle tore off, leaving us alone once more.

Dad turned to Mum. 'We don't have a car. All we possess is the baby's pram and a stroller.'

No sooner had the groan of the jeep disappeared in the dust, than Mum went into the house and handed each of us a sling bag. 'Put your clothes in. There'll be no luxuries from now on.'

Mum knew exactly what she wanted. She loaded the pram with blankets and warm clothes, then hurried to the kitchen to pack tins of condensed milk, cheese and corned meat in a cardboard carton. Grabbing the Gripe Water and Steedman's powder for Baby, she put them in a bag. From the medicine cabinet, she chose the blue jar of Vicks Vapour Rub and green tin of Zambuck ointment, the Murine eye drops, a bottle of iodine and a box of aspro. Finally, she snatched up the black velvet handbag containing her jewellery and a golden lacquer cylinder of important documents. She tucked them beneath the blankets and positioned her sewing case on the top.

She nodded to Rupert to take the pram.

She hesitated as she fondled the family photo album. Then she put it back on the shelf, before loading the stroller with clothes for Baby and herself. In went some packets of biscuits. Her little black prayer books and a mother-of-pearl rosary were last—her bastion of hope in times of despair.

Bertie stepped forward to push the stroller.

Dad grabbed his gun and ammunition. He slung a *dah* and a bag of personal items across his shoulders. The *dah* was a long silver-handled sword he had smuggled out from the Shan States during a holiday to Kalaw. Mum carried Rose, the medicines and food.

We joined the thickening stream of refugees heading towards the Irrawaddy River. Rupert's pram and Bertie's stroller were like mini battering rams, clearing a path for us through the throng. Dad grasped June's hand and Mum walked beside him with Baby in her arms. I clutched her dress, fearing the crowds pushing past would drag me away. I plodded along, my heart thumping.

June and I carried a blanket and a bag each. Herman's feeble arms were entwined around Nanny's neck. His withered and twisted legs dangled. His right arm, the only limb that could move, beat a tattoo on her back—a signaller sending out an SOS in Morse code. Whenever I walked within his reach, he snatched my hair.

Time seemed to disappear in the dusky silence and smoke. Even though winter was over, cold winds blew from the Himalayas. We wore several layers of clothes, and I felt like a stuffed toy. Clouds of dust stirred up by hurrying feet choked me and stung my eyes. My enchanted castle crashed to the ground.

A woman tore past, screaming. Two children ran bare-footed beside her—clothes blackened, bodies scorched and faces terror-stricken. A jagged piece of shrapnel protruded from her right shoulder, through her torn dress. Blood flowed down her arm and stained the soil bright red. I wanted to stop and help her. *Why did everyone keep their eyes fixed in front and not do something for the poor woman?*

They must have known the Japanese army was close behind. We fled towards the river, hoping to disperse among the villages on the opposite bank. The only alternative was to escape to the hills where tigers, leopards and *nats* lived.

'It's an evil place.' Nanny jerked her head. She had told us Buddhists believed in *nats*. These spirits sometimes took possession of a woman and gave her the power to cast spells on others—unless they placed offerings on their shrines.

I tightened my grip on Mum's dress and hurried along, afraid of the wild animals, the *nats*, the fire and, above all, the Japanese.

Chapter 5

The Refugee Camp

We arrived at the river, dusty and breathless. A launch belched smoke, preparing to leave. On its side, the name *Minthame* stood out in bold letters. 'What does that mean?' I asked June.

'Princess.'

Two crewmen were about to pull in the gangway when Dad requested a lift to the opposite bank. The captain beckoned us. We trod carefully on the plank, holding the rope railing. As we placed our belongings on the deck, I was aware of the strong smell of engine oil and a feeling of light headedness.

The captain bowed. 'I'm Nizami. *The Princess* is my boat. I'll take you across.' He gave us a cheery smile. The only smile I'd witnessed during the long, tedious day.

He left us for a few minutes and returned, balancing a plate as the launch leaped into motion. He placed the plate on a little folding table. 'Sorry, Madam. Doggie biscuits.' Then he left to shout directions to the crew.

Famished, I turned to Bertie. 'Is it safe to eat them?'

He smiled. 'Of course they're safe. The captain meant they are only fit for dogs because they're broken. He must have emptied his tin for us.'

I tucked in without waiting for Mum to nod her consent. Bertie took a biscuit, and soon Rupert and June joined us. We finished the lot by the time we had crossed the river.

Dad shook hands with Mr Nizami. 'Thank you so much for taking us across. We're on our way to a refugee camp. The Japs will confiscate your launch when they come. What will you do?'

'I intend to return to my home further downstream, collect my family and valuables, then fly out to India.'

Some thirty years later, Bertie revealed his fate with a catch in his voice. 'Mr Nizami was a wealthy mill-owner who was escaping from the Japs in his launch, *Minthame*. Not long after he took us across, Burmese *dacoits* robbed and killed him.' When I heard, the past floated before me once more and tears stung my eyes.

***

Dad hired two boatmen who were willing to take us to the refugee camp, fifteen kilometres upstream. The High Court's emergency plan for all Anglo-Indian and Anglo-Burmese staff was to meet at the village of Kyauktongyi. The English judges had already flown to India; Burmese employees had fled to their villages or to Buddhist monasteries.

Dad ordered Bertie to take one boat with all our belongings while the rest of us crowded into the other.

'I hope the boatman won't kill Bertie and rob our belongings,' Mum said. 'It doesn't matter so much if they steal our goods, as long as they leave Bertie behind and don't harm him. If they spare him and he keeps us in sight, he could run along the bank and join us when we get ashore. Bertie is such a resourceful boy.'

I couldn't see Bertie and was too terrified to turn around but Mum's words reassured me. I'd have been heartbroken if anything happened to him.

The boatman began rowing and we moved forward slowly against the current. Dad held his gun, pointing skywards. Mum gripped the sides—her knuckles white in the bright sun. June looked pale and wan. Rupert sat erect, like a sea captain in charge of everything.

The heavily laden canoe was close to the water line. Every time we shifted position, it tilted and even *I* sensed we were in danger from the slightest wave. Whenever it listed, we leaned in the opposite direction, trying to keep it on a steady keel.

'Don't rock the boat. Be still.' Dad's shouting only seemed to make things worse. Water splashed over the side and accumulated at the bottom, swishing among the floorboards. My shoes were wet.

The next movement would swamp us. *I knew it would.*

I clutched the hard wooden seats and stared straight ahead, trembling with a mixture of cold and fright. My teeth wouldn't stop chattering. A motor boat careered past, rocking our canoe. The boat's bow waves seemed like mountains of water pursuing us. The canoe shuddered. I couldn't shut out the sound of the splashing. I squeezed my eyes tight, waiting for the cold current to drag us to the depths of the dark swirling river.

'Start bailing.'

I opened my eyes at Rupert's shout. The water inside nearly reached the seats. The canoe rocked and took in more water. Rupert was using an empty condensed milk tin tied to a piece of string and attached to the keel for such an emergency. June was also bailing with one.

I cupped my hands to scoop up as much as I could and threw it over the side.

When we had bailed out most of the water, Rupert said, 'You may stop now.'

We turned our heads to look for Bertie's boat. The sun glinted on the river, blinding me. Nothing in sight. *Had he drowned?* Then I saw him far behind.

Still bailing, he glanced up and waved.

I waved back and licked my lips, longing for a drink.

The day was a cantankerous question mark set in an uncertain future. Time did not keep pace with the fast-flowing river. The trip seemed endless. Finally, the boatman rowed towards the bank and dragged the canoe to the river's edge. Trying not to slip on the wet floorboards, we clung on to each other and formed a chain to disembark.

Bertie's boat arrived a few minutes later.

Dad paid the two boatmen, then approached a villager and asked him to direct us to the refugee camp. The man led us along a dusty footpath through a jungle. A bamboo lookout tower stood at the entrance to the village. I discovered later a person took turns each night to watch for fires or *dacoits* and raise the alarm by striking a loud gong.

The huts huddled together as if trying to ward off the encroaching jungle. Dogs barked at us. Naked children ran around, unsupervised. Snot dribbled from their noses and flies swarmed over sores on their arms and legs. I stayed close to Mum. My stomach heaved at the thought of living in the wretched huts among the pi-dogs and dirty children.

Our guide walked ahead until he reached the edge of the village. Approaching a row of newly built huts, he stopped and spoke a few words to Dad. Then he left. 'He's gone to fetch the headman,' Dad said. 'He'll tell us which hut is ours.'

We stared at the huts. Male bamboo poles with solid centres supported the high-set dwellings. In the distance, a rooster crowed. The fresh smell of dung drifted in the evening air.

The headman arrived and held out his hand for a hundred rupees. The government had paid for the huts but he was intent on charging us as well.

Dad gave him the money without demur. 'It's better not to antagonise the villagers. We don't want to have our throats cut at night,' he explained to Mum.

We followed the headman to our new home. A brand-new hut awaited us, smelling of freshly cut bamboo. The floors were split female bamboo with hollowed centres, woven together to form a mat. Palm leaves served as tiles for the roof and strips of cane fastened everything down. No nails. The steps were lengths of bamboo tied together. They lacked a firm surface, so we had to be careful using the stairs.

Dad hired a villager to fetch water from the river. The man carried it in two kerosene oil tins suspended on each side from a bamboo yoke balanced on his shoulder. The tins bounced as he laboured to our hut and poured the contents into a large earthenware jar in the bathroom.

'Water is precious and costs money.' Mum rationed it, giving us each of us a couple of cups full for washing.

How I missed Rangoon where we only had to turn on a tap.

Sanitary conditions were even worse. It was simply a tiny hut built over a hole. Whenever I entered it, I took care not to fall into the gaping chasm where maggots squirmed in the excrement.

Life was difficult without piped water, proper toilets, showers, and electricity. I found the sudden change from comfortable city-life to the hardships and privations of village-life disturbing. As a consequence, I developed the habit of biting my left under-lip. The reasons for our constant upheavals eluded me. *Why were we staying in this cramped hut with not enough water to wash ourselves and no proper toilets?*

'Don't wear your shoes,' Dad said. 'Do you want to show that you are rich city folk? Do you want to be kidnapped or killed?'

So we went around barefooted. Splinters from the bamboo floor and thorns from the jungle embedded themselves in our feet. Mum extracted them with a sharp needle, after sterilising it in a candle flame.

'Hide your western dresses,' Dad said. 'Wear a *loongyi* like the native women so that you will remain hidden from Japanese patrols.'

Mum had trouble adjusting to her new garb and constantly tripped over. But she grew in strength through these difficulties—strength needed to face the tempestuous times ahead.

Kyauktongyi was in a malaria-infested area and each of us had to take a quinine tablet daily. Due to the medicine, our faces lost their coffee-with-milk shade and became saffron-coloured. We developed a ringing in our ears.

Someone had once boxed Rupert's left ear in a fight. He not only heard the ringing, but also grew partially and permanently deaf on that side.

***

Before our departure from Rangoon, the government had paid Dad six months' advance salary. He placed all the remaining bank notes in a piece of cloth which Mum sewed securely and tied around my belly. '*Dacoits* will never think a little child carries the family treasure,' Dad said.

I ate and slept with the money belt. It became part of my body, except when having a wash or a bath. The skin beneath the binding felt hot and itchy, but I dared not complain.

Throughout the war, the wad of notes grew slimmer and slimmer. At nights, I had trouble sleeping and lay awake, waiting for the sound of the gong warning us of *dacoits*. When dawn spread its first grey fingers over the sky and the chorus of birds and animals began shattering the stillness, Nanny would hustle us into the jungle. She brought a tiffin-carrier of food and a bottle of drinking water. The upper branches of the tall trees merged together and seemed to watch us malignantly. The jungle was silent but, at times, a cacophony of cicadas deafened us. The first time I heard it, the hairs on the nape of my neck rose.

Nanny chortled. 'Don't be afraid. It's only thousands of insects calling their wives.'

I glanced around, wide-eyed.

At times, monkeys chattered in the jungle. 'If you hear a monkey, you know a tiger's there too.' Nanny's warning did nothing to allay my fears. A sickening sensation rose in my belly.

'I need to go to the toilet,' I whimpered.

Nanny pulled a cut-up square of old newspaper from her Shan bag. 'Use this. We have no toilet paper here. In our village we use sticks.'

I gazed speechless as she gave us a demonstration on a piece of paper she'd shaped in the form of a human posterior. The boys looked at each other and laughed. Heat rose to my face and I longed for my cosy city-life.

When the sun threw long shadows upon the ground, we returned with thorns in our feet. But at least the daily trip into the jungle provided us the chance to remain outdoors. It was better than staying in a cramped hut the whole day like Mum.

The boys grew bored and went off for walks deep in the jungle. June, Herman and I picnicked alone with Nanny. In the evenings, Bertie would tell us of his walks in the bamboo forest and I begged him to take me along. One day he brought along a *dah*—a heavy knife something like an axe—and took me to an area where the bamboo was so thick he had to hack his way into the forest.

I told June about our adventure on my return. She smiled and led me a little way into the rainforest, away from the bamboo jungle. In the distance, I saw what looked like showers of gold. As we grew closer, I smelt their honeyed breath and inhaled the perfume of dark-leaved orchids with sprays of golden flowers. I thought I'd never seen anything so beautiful.

***

A few weeks later, signs of the impending downpour started to appear. Our excursions became all but impossible. Until the monsoons broke, Rupert took walks deep into the jungle to escape the monotony of our daily routine.

One day he failed to return before dark. We gathered around Mum and waited. *Had a tiger or a leopard taken him? Did he lose his way, or had a Japanese patrol seized him? Would he ever come home again?* I bit my lip.

When Rupert returned, Dad greeted him with a thick leather belt in his hand. 'Haven't I told you always to return *before* sunset? Get into the next room.'

Then he let fly with the belt.

Rupert took his punishment without a whimper. I heard the crack as the belt landed on his back, and shuddered with each blow. The sound ripped at my heart. Mum cringed in a corner, tears trembling on her lashes. June hid her face in her hands.

Bertie's features contorted in agony. 'He asked me to come along. I *told* him Dad would be angry.'

My father often belted the boys. Rupert always remained quiet, never uttering a sound.

Bertie was different. 'Sorry, Dad. I won't do it again,' he'd say, and Dad would stop.

Minutes passed. The thud of the belt sounded through the thin mat wall. I gave up counting. *Would Dad ever stop?*

His arm must have begun to tire. He stopped and stomped into his bedroom. The floor shook as he banged the door shut.

None of us dared tend Rupert's cuts, in case Dad punished us. We crept to bed. My mouth was dry as I drew up the blanket to my chin and covered myself, too afraid even to speak to June.

When Dad left the house for his daily walk next morning, we gathered around Rupert. It was the worst thrashing he'd ever received. The leather had ripped open his skin and torn into his back, leaving welts. Mum wept as she applied ointment.

Rupert bore the scars of this thrashing to his dying day, yet I never saw him show any resentment towards Dad.

Black clouds of anger filled me with bitterness and grew like a canker within me. I feared my father and, as time passed, I withdrew into my inner self, keeping out of his way whenever possible.

This fear and dislike of him grew with each succeeding year.

Chapter 6

My Family and Community

As the war progressed, my mother told us about herself. Orphaned at eighteen, she inherited a three-bedroom brick house in Mandalay and another three-bedroom home at Civil Lines on the outskirts of town. By 1922, she had obtained a Diploma in Teaching and taught at St. Joseph's School where she'd spent her student days. An ardent admirer, Joe, wanted to marry her—they quarrelled over a trifle and parted. In frustration, he joined a seminary. A year later, he realised the priesthood was not for him and returned—too late. She'd already married.

While Joe was away, mutual friends introduced my mother, May Scriven, to Esau White. He was the only son in a family of three children. Short of stature, with a soft voice, hawk-like nose and swarthy complexion, his charming manners attracted many women. Whenever my mother wore her white dress with lace trimmings, he praised her beauty and called her his *vision in white*. He drove a black Austin, and would bow as he opened her door when escorting her to the cinema. For the few months of their cyclonic courtship, she felt flattered by his attention.

At the time, she boarded at St Joseph's Convent. The nuns had strict rules prohibiting anyone from returning later than ten o'clock at night. One enthralling evening, time passed unnoticed. The iron gates were locked. She could have scrambled over, but the convent door too would be locked. What could she do?

She asked Esau to drive her over to a friend's place. There, she knocked at the door and begged for a night's shelter.

The next morning, a nun ushered her into the Mother Superior's office and ordered her to wait. Like a guilty student, my mother stood, shifting her weight from one foot to the other, her heart pounding.

The Mother Superior entered, bringing a draught of cold air with her. 'May Scriven! I am surprised at you. Your father's dying wish was for you to remain in our care. You've broken the rules and there's nothing I can do but send you away. May God have mercy on your soul!'

My mother left the room with that curt order echoing in her ears. Packing her things, she returned to her girl friend's place. She had stayed away from the convent for the whole night, so she'd lost her good name. No one, except her girlfriend, would believe she had not spent the night with Esau.

As he drove her from the convent, tears cascaded down her face. Neither of her parents was alive; she had no one to turn to. Her only option was to marry Esau. She wiped her eyes and gazed at him.

He drove to a quiet spot and turned off the ignition. 'You know I adore you. I'll do anything; even marry you in church, if you'll have me.' He'd been brought up a Muslim, but he practised no religion.

She nodded. There was no alternative. 'We must see Father Dan, my Parish Priest, and hear what he has to say.'

Without a word, he started the car and drove to the presbytery.

***

The sound of the wheels on the gravelled drive must have alerted the priest to visitors. He met the couple at the door and showed them in. The waiting room was sparsely furnished with a desk and chairs. A crucifix hung on the wall behind his desk.

He shook hands and gestured for them to be seated. He listened in silence before rising from his chair. Standing with his hands on his hips, he towered over Esau. 'I'll allow you to marry in church, provided you promise to bring up your future offspring as Catholics.'

'I refuse to have them brought up as Catholics. The most I can do is to assure you that they will never be *forced* to join any religion. Children are too young to know their minds. They may make their own choice when they grow up.'

The priest shook his head and looked at my mother. 'In that case, I cannot marry you.'

She gasped. Esau grabbed her hand and stormed out of the presbytery.

Mum turned and glanced back in sorrow at the priest. She could no longer board at the convent, nor impose further on her friend, who had recently married. The priest would not marry her in church and she could not face a life ostracised by society.

Even though the church would not recognise her marriage, she would be legally wed if she married in the law-courts.

She consented to that option.

***

After marriage, my father revealed a jealous nature. He frequently slapped my mother, accusing her of trying to attract other men. At other times, he treated her with unparalleled grace, as though his cruelty was merely a side-effect of his all-consuming love.

We were born in Mandalay—the city made famous by Rudyard Kipling. I didn't know then what joy his *Jungle Books* would later bring. We lived in Civil Lines, a row of fine houses in an elite suburb where many British officials and executives resided. Our house nestled in a large garden with velvety lawns, all cared for by our *mali*, an Indian gardener who came in daily.

The year I was born, Rupert had just turned five and Bertie four. June was not yet three. Mum was afflicted by a racking cough and doctors thought she had consumption. So Nanny took care of Rupert, Bertie, June and me in another part of the house.

After a few months, the doctor realised his mistake and, to Mum's joy, Dad allowed us to return to her. During the period of separation I'd bonded with my nanny, and cried whenever Mum attempted to caress me. Mum tried to amuse me and showed me picture books, but I would not return her affections until she discharged Nanny.

Two years after my birth, Dad was transferred to Rangoon. We left

Mandalay and moved into government quarters. Our new home had a garage and servants' quarters at the back. The large lounge room, dining room and kitchen were downstairs. Upstairs were our bedrooms, the bathroom and toilet. The balcony overlooking the stairs served as our playroom.

The two-storeyed brick stucco building was identical to all the other whitewashed houses. Only the front yards looked different.

In this early period of my life, I can only recall that Mum missed her hometown.

My memory goes back to my third year. Dad worked in the High Court as a secretary, going to work in his white tropical suit. On his return in the evenings, he'd tell Mum of his day. To protect us from prowlers, he forbade us from playing in the garden after dark. There was no television in those days; Rupert read in his room and Bertie sang as he painted.

Dad sank into his easychair, drank a bottle of stout and smoked his pipe. June, who sat at Dad's feet, would ask him to blow smoke rings for her. We'd watch them drift up to the ceiling.

I sprawled on the carpet near Mum and listened to the radio. Young as I was at the time, it seemed to me that, confident of his skills and highly competitive, Dad's brusque and belligerent manner made office boys cringe and obey him.

He ordered the *peon* to carry his files and follow him home, a ten-minute-walk from the High Court. On these occasions, the *peon* followed Dad into the lounge and laid the files on a table. Dad always turned away without a word, and the office boy bowed and *salaamed* to his back.

Mum had taught us to thank people when we received a favour, so I often wondered why Dad never thanked him.

Fellow workers kept their distance, but senior officials and judges relied on Dad for his efficiency. He'd boast whenever a judge selected him to tour the district courts. 'Justice Mosley chose me and passed over D'Cruz,' he'd tell Mum. 'I'm afraid I'll be away for a couple of weeks.'

On reflection, I realise that Dad's aggressive energy drove him.

***

I was delighted whenever Dad was on tour, because Mum let us play with our neighbours' children. Sometimes, on moonlit nights, she even allowed us to join the games in front of our house. She said no harm would come to June or me as long as we remained with Rupert and Bertie. So from then on, whenever my brothers were around, I never feared anything.

When Dad was away, Mum reminisced about her past. 'My grandfather left England to work as a guard on the Madras Railways in India. While stationed at Bangalore, he married Mabel Locke. With the prospect of promotion, my grandparents moved to Burma where my dad, George Scriven, was born. When he had completed his education, he too worked on the Burma railways. Later, he married my mum, Rose Mariano, a fervent Catholic of Portuguese descent.'

'Do you have any brothers, Mummy?' June asked.

'I've two brothers.' Mum gazed at Rupert and Bertie. 'George is seven years my junior and Pat a couple of years younger than him. When my father died of pneumonia at thirty-six, my mother received a large sum of money from his Provident Fund. She remarried twelve months after his death and, feeling she should've remained loyal to Dad, I was hurt.' A sigh shook Mum.

'Before another year had passed, my mother died after giving birth to twins. Only one survived. My stepfather needed someone to care for his young child, and married Alice, a friend of mine. We were both eighteen.'

Mum paused, a faraway look in her eyes. 'George and Pat were sent as boarders to St. Peter's. I was married to your dad by then and during the first years of my marriage they spent the summer holidays with me. When they reached their teens, your Dad couldn't put up with them, so they had to go to our step-father instead. After they completed their education, George joined the priesthood. Pat worked on the railways.'

She lifted the photo album from the shelf. 'My dad had a magnificent military bearing. Bertie has taken after him—especially his nose. Your grandpa was fair-haired and blue-eyed, strong and muscular, with a deep voice.'

Grandfather stared at us from the page. I noticed his broad forehead. *Yes, Bertie did look a bit like him.*

I can still see Bertie winding up the gramophone and imitating Bing Crosby and opera tenors like Caruso. He frequently sat mixing watercolours and painting pictures for us, all the while humming a tune or singing a song. He carried a mouth organ in his pocket and played it often. He sang away heartaches with his soothing voice, and was always the first to forgive an injury or help anyone in need.

Rupert and June were fond of books. Rupert spent all his allowance on them and invariably received one for Christmas and birthdays. He would shut himself in his room, devouring a book. He also had a genius for raising cash.

One Christmas, Santa brought Rupert a film projector. A week later, he drew the curtains, and invited us to watch films for one *pice*—about the equivalent of a farthing. He stood at the doorway and collected the money from each of us. Then he showed films of *Charlie Chaplin, Tarzan* and *The Three Stooges*. I was glued to the seat, my eyes fixed on the screen.

Afterwards, Rupert counted the takings and set off for the nearest bookstore. When he ran out of money, he resorted to any means to buy more books. If cash went missing, he was the first under suspicion. We had a large red cedar safe with ornate brass-handled drawers, where Mum deposited all her coins. It contained her jewellery and Dad's savings. Mum called it her locker.

When I was little, she often held me over a slot on the top of the locker and I'd drop in the change Cook handed her on his return from the bazaar. I loved to hear the *chink* of the coins as they fell to the bottom.

I saw some cash on the table one day and, fetching a chair, I climbed it, listening for the jingle as I let each coin fall.

A few minutes later, I heard the muffled sound of Mum's voice.

'I didn't take it,' Rupert shouted.

I ignored the drama, as he was always in trouble.

A sudden thought must have struck Mum, because she left him and rushed to me. 'Was any money lying here this morning?'

'Yes. I put it away for you.'

She scratched her head. 'How did you reach the top?'

Proud of what I'd done, I carried a chair to the safe, clambered up and stretched across to the slot.

Once upstairs, I laughed with the relief of getting away. 'Rupert passed wind just now.' Mum had taught us not to use the word 'fart'. Every time we smelled one, though, we'd glance at each other and giggle with embarrassment.

Bertie chuckled. 'Lucky Dad didn't hear Rupert.'

'Poor Mummy's getting a beating. How can you laugh about it?' June said.

Bertie flushed. Rupert had already returned to his books.

***

Within two years of the move from Mandalay, Herman was born with infantile paralysis. He could sit but never learned to crawl. When he neither walked nor talked, Dad took him to a specialist.

The clinic smelt of antiseptic like carbolic soap. The nurse ushered us into a room and placed Herman on a bed with snowy white sheets. Then she strapped him down. The white-gowned doctor ran a gadget along his arms and legs.

Herman's limbs twitched, his eyes rolled, his lips trembled and he strained against the straps. I expected him to get up and talk, but although his whole mouth moved, no sound issued forth.

Mum moaned.

It made me wonder whether the current went through her too.

Every day we searched for signs of improvement but Herman didn't get better even after the third treatment. When the electric shock therapy failed, Dad sent for my old nanny to care for him. I couldn't remember her but Mum told me of my attachment to her, so I waited eagerly for her arrival.

Dad drove to the station to fetch her. She lived in Mandalay, and travelled down to Rangoon by train on receiving my parent's letter.

As soon as I heard our car pull into our driveway, I rushed out to meet her. Nanny held out her arms to me. I just gaped. Betel-juice had stained her remaining teeth a reddish brown. Her hair was the colour of ash. Only the smell of sandalwood was familiar. I'd imagined her to be young and beautiful.

Nanny fed my brother, cleaned him when he soiled his pants and bathed him. Herman became totally dependent on her.

Mum rushed back to Rupert. 'I'm so sorry, son. I thought you'd taken it.'

She was deeply remorseful about the accusation and brought up the matter years later. Mum never could forgive herself and often said she had not been kind and patient with him.

***

I remember racing downstairs to open the front door for Dad on his return from work.

'Take off my shoes,' he'd say, and throw himself on a chair. Then he'd place a leg over my shoulder as I sat on the floor.

I unlaced his shoes, pulled them off and rolled down his damp and smelly stockings.

'Careful now,' he'd warn me. 'Don't pull my hairs.'

June said his stockings reeked of 'toe-jam', but glad to please him, I put up with the smell.

My father generally hid his brutality from us, and Mum never mentioned her sufferings. One weekend, however, the shroud of secrecy lifted. The servants had retired to their quarters, and we were upstairs having our afternoon nap.

Rupert's voice woke me. 'Come quickly. Daddy is belting Mummy.' He waved his arms and pointed downstairs.

I followed Rupert, Bertie and June as they tiptoed to the dining room. The lounge room door was ajar. Rupert crawled under a table. Bertie, June and I followed, and peered from behind him.

My parents were standing, facing each other. Two imprints of a hand showed on Mum's pale cheeks. They were nearly as red as the carpet. Dad was shouting, and Mum was weeping. She inched towards the centre table, as if to position the glass tulips as a barrier between them.

I bit my lip and hunched even lower. The image of Mum's face remains imprinted on my mind.

Rupert broke wind. Bertie held his nose as we reversed out of the room. Hearts racing, we scampered up the stairs. We knew if Dad saw us, he'd probably beat us too.

We all considered him a burden and left him entirely to Nanny's care. Everyone continued to treat me as the baby of the family.

If the weather was fine, Nanny took June and me for a stroll in the evenings. 'Hold hands. You're crossing the street,' she'd say.

The park was not far from our home. June always turned the walk into an exciting activity. My soul vibrated with music, like a harp, whenever she plucked on its strings. We picked frangipani, felt the velvet softness of its petals, inhaled deeply. Heading for the rotunda, she would make believe and take me to some far-off place on her magic carpet. Sounds of others playing grew remote as we rambled in a world of our own.

Nanny steered us away from other children, observing the taboos of society in those days. Europeans did not socialise with the natives, nor did Anglo-Indians mingle with others. Eurasians—the Anglo-Indians and Anglo-Burmese contemptuously described as *cafe au lait*—lived like the genuine *sahib*, but on a minor scale. We attended English schools, conversed in English and only spoke Burmese or Hindustani to our servants.

Too young to understand the social structure in Burma, I still automatically obeyed the unwritten rules. Prior to the war, the class system—similar to the caste system of India, but more subtle—had many tiers. The governor stood at the pinnacle, and below him were senior officials—mostly British, with a sprinkling of highly educated Burmese. European employees of large companies and banks were next in line. British timbermen, oil engineers and rubber plantation owners came after them, followed by European missionaries.

Indians were wealthy merchants, tradespeople, coolies or domestics. Japanese chose to work as doctors, dentists or photographers, while three hundred thousand Chinese lived in Chinatown, going about their own business.

All this changed after the war.

Before the outbreak of hostilities, the *dhobi* delivered our neatly ironed clothes, and took away the soiled linen once a week. Mum recorded each item in a large red book and supervised the *jadu wallah* who came in daily to clean the bathroom and toilet. The two rooms always smelled of phenol.

We also had a cook who had served an English family. They had trained him well, and we reaped the benefits. He not only cooked the most delicious meals but dished them up with flair. A bowl of Irish stew would be accompanied by mashed potatoes forming a circle on the inner circumference of the serving dish.

Among all our servants, Cook remained my favourite—perhaps because he served such tasty meals. Each morning, Mum gave him a shopping list for fresh meat, fruit and vegetables. On his return from market, Mum selected the day's menu.

While Nanny looked after Herman, Mum supervised the household, sewed dresses or made curtains for the house. She often sat on her rocker with a book or a journal. A romantic, she especially liked *True Story* magazine.

We lived a comfortable lifestyle at Rangoon. Mum's grand piano had belonged to her mother but I never saw her sit at it, even though she loved music and sang most days.

'I don't use it anymore.' Mum was apologetic when I asked her to play something for me. 'It's out of tune and Daddy won't call the piano-tuner in to fix it. He says it makes me think of my old days.'

I was only three then and wondered why he objected to her thinking of the past. Whenever he was out and the radio played a waltz, Mum would dance across our sitting room. Her eyes lit up as she beamed at us. She had won prizes in ballroom dancing but I never saw any of her trophies.

Dancing was one of the many pleasures Mum had to give up after marriage. When I was in my teens, she told me Dad had said, 'Men only dance to have the pleasure of pressing themselves against women.'

***

Even as a very young child, I realised Dad regulated what we did and who we associated with. More often than not, he only let us mix with his nieces and nephews.

On rainy days, we went to the pictures after lunch at our aunt's and uncle's place. Mum allowed us to bathe at their house before we returned home. We only had a shower rose at home. I half-filled the great white porcelain tub and soaked in the foamy suds until Mum called out to hurry.

I remember going to the *Wizard of Oz*, *Snow White and the Seven Dwarfs* and *Shirley Temple* movies. Only once did I go along to a Gary Cooper film. I loved the cowboys, the shooting, the swing doors in the bars and the Red Indians with their feathered headdresses and tomahawks.

'Your father is like that actor,' Mum said, as we drove home.

I took a small intake of breath in surprise. Dad wasn't tall or good-looking. I disliked his hooked nose and deep-set eyes, and questioned his resemblance to Gary Cooper.

***

We invariably spent New Year's Day at the Rangoon Show-grounds. One of my earliest memories is a military parade held there. June sat astride Dad's shoulders and I perched on Mum's. Even now, the touch of her soft hands returns to me. I see her large, light brown eyes, her cupid bow lips, pale skin and freckled cheeks which, she said, the fairies had sprinkled with gold dust.

I gazed in rapture at the colours flying, soldiers marching, cavalry prancing and horse-drawn gun-carriages, while the bands played *Rule Britannia*. I smelled the odour of perspiration from the men and horses, even though it was winter.

We went to the parade ground every New Year's Day until the Japanese bombed Rangoon. The invasion commenced less than a week after the bombing of Pearl Harbour. The enemy attacked Tavoy, a British military outpost south of Rangoon. The next day, on 12 December, small Japanese units began infiltrating Burma. Three days later, Japan's Fifteenth Army landed at Victoria Point, Burma's southernmost tip.

My parents heard all this on the news.

I knew nothing of it at the time.

***

I cannot remember Dad's father. I was only two at the time we left Mandalay for Rangoon. He owned a garage and sold second-hand cars. My father used to borrow the black Austin when he courted my mother. After their marriage, he bought it from his father.

Dad traded in the Austin for a maroon Chevrolet when our family increased in size. It had automatic indicators. The plush seats gave off a pleasant odour and aroused a feeling of grandeur.

When Grandfather died and his funeral was over, Grandmother boarded a train to Rangoon and moved into our home. She was like a barrel of beer—short and fat. Several times a day, she wore a white garment and prayed in a strange language. She'd adopt peculiar positions—she'd sit on her bed on her knees, sometimes placing her forehead on the pillow, sometimes standing.

She never spoke to Mum but shadowed her like a ghost, hiding in corners and behind doors to spy on her. In the evenings, she reported to Dad the names of everyone who'd entered our home during his absence.

Once when Rupert, Bertie and June were at school, Mum invited a pedlar in. His goods were packed in two squares of cloth hung on a bamboo pole. He squatted on the floor, laid down his bundles and arranged the articles before us. Ribbons of all colours, reels of coloured thread, buttons of all shapes and sizes, laces and silk dresses lay displayed on the two squares.

I gazed in fascination as Mum picked up a pink frock with a honeycomb pattern below the yoke and at the sleeves. She placed it against me and put it aside, then chose a honey-coloured dress with smocking and silk-embroidered flowers for June.

That evening when Dad returned from work, his mother hurried over to him. She pointed at Mum, spoke excitedly and threw up her arms.

Dad strode up and slapped Mum, leaving a bright red mark on her face. She attempted to explain, but her mother-in-law turned her back and, pulling up her *loongyi*—sarong, bent over to expose her rump.

I stared. My muscles tensed and my hands flew to my face. I gawked at the venerable old woman's huge buttocks.

Mum gasped and put her hand over my eyes. Although I was only three at the time, the spectacle haunted me. I longed for revenge, despite all Mum's entreaties to forgive and forget.

The following evening, when Dad was still in the office, Rupert chased Bertie across Grandmother's room while she was at prayer. They ran in one door and out the other, the floor resounding to their shouting and thumping feet.

I wondered what Bertie had done to make Rupert so angry and hoped he wouldn't thrash him.

As they passed me, Bertie winked. I realised then they were harassing Grandmother to teach her not to sneak about Mum.

They were heroes in my childish eyes.

Grandmother never again told tales. Neither did she report their behaviour to Dad. She adored his sons and remained silent. Like most Muslims, she considered men far superior to women. She continued to live with us until Rangoon was bombed.

That was the one good the bombing did for us.

Chapter 7

School Days

When my sister was at school, the days were long and lonely. I'd sit by the window, both palms flattened against the pane, watching the rain falling in sheets. I marvelled at the sight of a dark sky suddenly lit by lightning, the sounds of thunder, and branches blown along the roads. Rivers of water flowed into the storm-water drains.

In the afternoons, around 3 o'clock, I'd rush to the gate and crane my neck to look down the road. I was eager for June to return and play with me on the seesaw or with our dolls. I scarcely missed my brothers. I was too young to join them playing ball, having a game of marbles, spinning their tops or shooting crows with their catapults.

June's first words to me were always: 'Found any sweets today?'

I'd shake my head.

'Look for them. The fairies left some for you.'

I'd run around searching until I discovered a sweet wrapped in cellophane hidden among my toys. But even the delight of rolling a lolly on my tongue did not lessen the pain of parting from her each morning.

Mum read me stories of knights in shining armour, sending me off to a world of fun and fantasy. She taught me to read the words from picture books long before I started school, and I soon graduated to Anderson's fairy tales. The more proficient I became, the more I enjoyed reading.

Mum taught me how to hold a pencil. I still feel her gentle touch as she guided my faltering hand. I painstakingly practised the letters until

I could write the whole alphabet. One hot and humid evening, June sat beside Dad with her exercise book. He whispered praise to her. I waited slate in hand to show him what I'd done during the day. My damp hand smudged the writing. My legs ached from standing so long on the cold concrete floor. I shuffled my feet and wiped my clammy hands on my dress, careful not to erase the work.

Dad stood and turned away without glancing at me.

My heart shrank, my chest tightened. I stumbled towards June, raised the slate and struck her head. The slate broke into two pieces.

What had I done?

I stepped back and stared.

Her eyes opened wide in surprise.

Dad spun around. 'Come here.'

I toddled over and stood tight-lipped before him.

'Why did you do that?' His voice sounded like thunder.

Overcome by fear of the impending punishment, I bit my lip and swallowed hard. I tasted salt.

'Don't *ever* do it again.'

I looked down, not daring to say anything.

His voice rose. 'Do you hear me?'

I nodded.

'Hold out your hand.' He picked up a ruler and struck my hand. Two stinging bites left red welts. A painful lump rose in my throat. I ran to my dolls, put them in a circle around me and hugged Toddles. June had named my rag doll after our cuddly white pup a car had run over.

Later on that day, I asked her to play with me.

'Why did you hit me?'

I hung my head. 'I don't know.'

She forgave me instantly.

***

I commenced school at the beginning of the new term, in May, when I turned four. A warm feeling rose within me. I once more had June close, even though we were in different classes.

During the morning tea break, June introduced me to a little boy named Lazarus. 'His sister and I are friends. He'll look after you.'

My brothers and cousins were the only boys I knew. I smiled shyly. His eyes glistened and his jet-black hair was neatly combed back. I liked his long, curly lashes, but his name irked me. It reminded me of the story of Lazarus, who had sores all over his body and ate scraps that fell from the rich man's table.

We rarely spoke at first. For the next few days we spent the latter half of our lunch hours together, walking about in the playground.

Our friendship terminated when he played a boyish prank on me. 'Hazel, look here.' He held his pencil close to my eye.

I turned towards him. The pencil missed my eyeball by a fraction of a centimetre, nearly blinding me. It left an angry, red mark. Tears filled my eyes, obscuring my vision. I covered my eye with my hand. It ached, but the greater pain was to think a trusted friend had done this to me.

The scar on my sclera remains to this day, a constant reminder to be wary of trusting others until they have proved themselves—so at least something good turned up from our brief acquaintance.

After dire threats to Lazarus, warning him to stay away from me, June introduced me to Sheila Archer, a girl with curls like Shirley Temple. An only child and a year older than me, she took everything seriously. We became dear friends and sat next to each other in class. Reading time brought us closer together as we adored books. By then I already read well, but I still found it difficult to hold a pencil correctly.

At lunchtimes, Sheila preferred to sit and talk rather than play, so I sacrificed my love of games and we chatted instead. When her birthday drew close, Sheila invited me to her party. I couldn't wait for the end of the school day and jumped and skipped all the way back. June had to restrain me from running.

'May I go, Mummy? What present should I take? She's my best friend.' I hardly paused for breath.

Mum brushed back my hair with her hand. 'You must get Daddy's permission first. He'll be back shortly. Ask him after he's changed his clothes.'

On his return, Dad kissed Mum and, giving a low growl of acknowledgement to our greeting, went upstairs to change into something more comfortable.

As soon as he came down, I crept up to him with the question trembling on my lips.

'What do you want?' he snapped.

'My best friend … Sheila … at school.'

'Sheila! Who's she?'

'My friend. We do everything together.'

'What about her?' He picked up the newspaper and scanned the headlines.

'Her birthday is on Saturday and she's invited me to her party.'

He slammed down the paper. 'What?'

'May I please go, Daddy?'

'No!' His gaze was withering. 'You must not go. There'll be boys, and they'll teach you things.' He turned away and buried his face in his newspaper.

'Please, Daddy.'

'No. Never. And stop sniffling right now.'

Too afraid to plead any longer and confused by his words, I raced to my mother. 'Mummy. He won't let me go. He said there'll be boys at the party and they'll teach me things.'

'Evil be who evil thinketh.' Mum enfolded me in her arms.

The following day, I hesitated before breaking the news to my friend. Then I blurted out, 'Dad won't allow me to go to your party.'

Sheila stood speechless. Her face dropped. She walked away and out of my life. Our blossoming friendship drooped and died like an unwatered plant. I knew I'd let her down, but there was nothing I could do. Inwardly, I blamed my father and never forgave him. I no longer sat at his feet to remove his shoes and socks. Even now, a flame of anger leaps to my breast at the thought of his severity.

One good resulted from the alienation, however. I was free to play with other girls during lunch times. I played *Salts*, trying to cross the chalked line without anyone catching me. I took part in cricket, batting with fierce determination and endeavouring to catch the ball when the opposing team batted. I indulged in rough games like *Thief and Police*, hanging on with an inescapable hold, as Rupert and Bertie had taught me.

June not only found me companions at school, she also protected me against bullies.

'The girls won't let me join them in their games,' I complained one day.

My sister scowled and clenched her fist. 'I'll teach them a lesson.'

The next morning, she accosted the leader, Gladys. June placed her hand on the girl's chest and shoved her. 'Why don't you let Hazel play?'

Gladys staggered back. I flushed with pride. How brave my sister was! Gladys was about June's age and surrounded by friends, yet my brave sister had dared to take her on.

Again, June pushed her. Gladys did not attempt to fight and something must have told my sister she had won, for she turned to me. 'Go on then.'

I shuffled forward apprehensively.

Gladys gave her friends a nod and they immediately accepted me into their circle. The incident served to bond me with June even closer.

***

Our routine seldom varied in those halcyon days before the war. In the mornings, Mum dressed me for school. June and I wore Dad's old neckties Mum had altered for us. I found it difficult to tie a Windsor knot, but she stood behind me in front of a mirror and helped me master the intricate process.

Although we had servants, Mum insisted we make our beds before leaving for school. We grumbled. 'Why doesn't Nanny do it for us?'

'We never know what may happen in the future. Perhaps some day you won't be able to keep servants. Then what would you do?'

Rupert protested. 'But Nanny is here now and she has nothing better to do.'

Mum pinned him down with her schoolteacher's stare.

He dropped his eyes and returned to his room to make his bed. Bertie followed.

'Oh, Mum!' June dropped her school bag and went back to our bedroom.

I ran upstairs behind her and leaned over my bed, crushing my well-ironed navy blue tunic with its high yoke and three large box pleats. I finally succeeded in drawing up the coverlet to hide the rumpled sheet. Then I adjusted my belt. The white blouse remained without any creases, but my tie had slipped out from beneath the gymslip and needed adjusting too.

I sometimes recall my first attempts at bed-making and thank my mother now for teaching us not to rely on our servants to do *all* the work.

Within a few years, we had to do everything for ourselves.

***

Cook took us to school in the mornings. It was only a five-minute walk from our home in 46th Street to the Branch Convent in Judah Ezekiel Street. At lunch times, he returned with a three-tiered tiffin-carrier to the lunchroom. One tier contained rice, another a curry. The last had lentils. Cook spread a white cloth, then laid the table with care, as though June and I were back home in our dining room. He opened the tiffin-carrier, showing as much flair as a waiter at the Savoy, served us our luncheon and stood by.

Other children, too, sat eating in the large hall with its rough benches and tables while their servants waited. The nuns kept us in such a state of awe we ate in silence. Nothing could be heard but the noise of passing traffic, the tinkle of cutlery, Sister's soft footsteps and the clink of the large black rosary she wore around her waist.

After we'd eaten, Cook folded the tablecloth and serviettes, put away the plates and returned home to prepare our evening meal.

Our school day started with morning prayers at 9.00 sharp, when the bell rang, heralding assembly. We lined up on the verandah. A concrete floor with concrete shamrock balusters supported the hand railings. The principal, Mother Emma, an elderly Irish nun from the Good Shepherd Order, glided to the front. Her eyes roved over us.

I knew she was checking the length of our uniforms, because she once called up a student and made her kneel before the whole assembly. As the girl's gymslip failed to touch the floor when she knelt, Mother Emma clicked her tongue. 'I'm asking your teacher to send a note home to your mother, requesting her to take down the hem.'

Few girls dared to wear short skirts after that, but the more daring ones would hitch their uniforms to a fashionable length.

The balcony became a nightmare when the monsoon was at its peak and gale-force winds beat on the tiled roof. We moved closer to the wall, away from the outer edge, but our clothes turned damp and cold. The rain created so much mist it was like standing at the base of a waterfall. I usually succeeded in securing a place next to the inner wall, perhaps because I was small and could easily slip between the mass of students. Even then, the cold air found its way down my neck, sending shivers along my spine. I tried to bundle myself into a ball.

Once assembled, we knelt and bowed our heads in prayer. I hoped it would be short as my knees ached from the cold hard floor. At the close of prayers everyone sang *Come, Holy Ghost, send down those Beams*. I'd glance up as the wind and rain battered the roof, wondering if the beams would collapse on us.

After the hymn, we rose to our feet and rubbed our knees. The principal paused until we stood at attention. She cleared her throat and called one of the students to stand beside her. I wondered whether the girl was going to be scolded, but Mother Emma proclaimed her a perfect model for the rest of us to follow.

As the chosen one strutted up, the principal pointed out the girl wore the correct tie and belt and had her hair tied back neatly in plaits. Like a fashion show.

I failed to understand why Mother Emma never chose me as a model. I reached out for acknowledgement, unaware of my standing within the Catholic community, too young to grasp that the nuns looked unfavourably upon children of a mixed marriage. They selected the school captain and class prefects from Catholic students and particularly favoured those who had Irish backgrounds.

Mum must have been aware of the stigma attached to us, since she had not married in Church, but she told us that we were just as good as the others.

Only later did I realise the prejudice and discrimination that occurred in institutions during that period.

At the final assembly of the year, Mother Emma extolled girls who had obtained the highest grades. She read out the names of top students from every class, and presented each of them with a medal.

Some tossed their heads like flighty horses as they minced up to the principal. Others swaggered up, their lips forming a half-sneer, half-smile.

June was invariably the top student in her grade. She stepped out, each step slow and deliberate. No sign of haughtiness or false modesty appeared as she took her place among the school's best students.

I straightened my shoulders and threw up my head whenever June's name was called to receive her medal. The principal never called me up as I was only second in class. Although I did not realise it then, it was a great credit to me, as most girls in my grade were at least a year or two older.

Apple Fernandez, who knelt in front during morning prayers, held first position in class. She never failed to fill me with resentment. Her shadow seemed a blight, trying to push me into the background, as if she were the only light worthy to shine in the room. I knew my rival obstructed any chances of ever achieving a medal. As we knelt in prayer in the mornings, I hoped Apple would fall ill and miss her exams. Then *I'd* obtain the highest marks and gain recognition. I longed for some sort of praise. Just a little medal, please God, I prayed.

To my chagrin, the sports teacher never selected me to play in the basketball team either. My shoulders drooped, and I lowered my head. I was the youngest and smallest girl in class and didn't stand a chance among girls so much taller and stronger than me.

***

We learned all the latest songs from Bertie, and often used to sing with June.

One day at school, my teacher, Miss Sequeria, beckoned me over. 'See me at lunch-time soon after you've had lunch. I've chosen you and five others to take part in the annual concert.'

Filled with excitement at being chosen, I hurried through my lunch and kept looking at the clock in the dining room.

Miss Sequeria taught me to sing and dance to *Umbrellas*. Mum made me practise every day until I knew the steps and the words of the song by heart. Before long, my confidence grew and my timidity decreased.

Mum and Dad came to the concert. The principal occupied the front row beside the bishop, who wore a ring with a large jewel on the second finger of his right hand. Our parents sat a few rows behind the distinguished guests.

June was a Red Indian and did a war dance with students from her class. Because of her grace in dancing and her delightful voice, the lay teachers always chose her to participate in the annual school concerts on St. Patrick's Day.

When my turn came, I shot a glance at my parents. Dad sat back, watching the other girls. Mum's eyes were fixed on me. At the end of the item, Mum almost jumped out of her seat as she clapped. Her flushed face shone even brighter than the rose-coloured stone on the bishop's hand.

***

On our return from school in the afternoons, we'd polish our leather shoes or clean our white tennis ones with Blanco if it happened to be a sports day. Then we sat down for a cup of Ovaltine and a slice of buttered bread and jam.

After we had changed and showered, Mum supervised our studies. 'What did the teacher give you for homework, Hazel?'

I recited my times-tables and poetry to Mum each afternoon. She'd tell me to sit down and study while she made sure Rupert, Bertie and June did their allocated studies. Only after we'd completed the work did she let us go out and play in the garden.

On rainy days, we all gathered around her for stories. She read the exciting scenes aloud and related the rest of the story in her own words. An excellent storyteller, her voice animated the characters and aroused my empathy. *Daddy Long Legs*, *Rebecca of Sunnybrook Farm*, *The Prince and the Pauper*, *Ivanhoe* and *Les Miserables* imprinted themselves on my mind.

We listened in rapt attention until Dad returned from work and we drifted off to dream of life in the world lying beyond our reach.

Chapter 8

Summer Holidays

When I was three, we left for Calcutta on the *SS Egra* for a trip to Darjeeling. I remember holding Mum's hand tightly as we climbed the gangway. Mum told us we'd be on the ship for days and it was to be our home for a time. I squealed with delight.

After a day at sea, the muddy water turned a beautiful emerald green, before changing to an inky blue. I imagined that, if we carried the water home and filled our inkbottles, we could sell them as ink and make a fortune. When I told Bertie my thoughts, he took me to the back where two seamen were drawing up buckets of sea-water to bathe. The water was colourless! I gazed in wonder at the change, and shook my head.

A terrible storm arose and rocked our vessel as it crossed the Indian Ocean. Would we, like Sinbad, be shipwrecked and have to live on an island? The wind howled and the sails flapped. Mum glanced up at them, shut her eyes and covered her ears. As I huddled against her and hoped we wouldn't drown, she threw up. June took my hand and led me away.

Rupert and Bertie took us all over the ship. They stopped and watched the engine, which was in an iron cage like the lions in the zoo. The odour of oil and the engine's heat and hissing was frightening. I grew hot and my breathing became short and fast so we went on deck to count the waves.

Dad disappeared somewhere on board the ship, but I scarcely missed him. I cannot recall how long Mum remained in bed, but one morning we awoke to find the sea had turned from sapphire to turquoise. The ship rode smoothly once more.

'Tell Mummy we're safe now,' Bertie said.

June and I ran off to deliver the good news. Mum rose from bed and had a shower and breakfast before joining us at the rails. I leaned against her, and felt as if a great weight had been lifted from my shoulders.

***

We arrived at Calcutta the next day. After a sea voyage of two weeks, I felt myself rocking and rolling when we disembarked. The traffic was thick and noisy, the weather hot and steamy, and cows wandered on the streets.

After we had checked in at a hotel, Dad took us to a large department store. Mum asked me to find something I wanted for my birthday. I headed straight for a display of dolls. Hundreds stood on a shelf, all asking for a home. They were so beautiful. I hesitated. Then my eyes lit upon a doll with baggy trousers, holding a walking stick. We had been to a Charlie Chaplin movie a few months before. Mum stood beside me and sang softly:

Now the sun shines bright on Charlie Chaplin,
His boots are cracking
For want of blacking…

Mum picked up the doll and wound a little key on its back. It walked towards me in short, jerky movements.

I threw my arms around her. 'I love this.'

She smiled. 'Go and look at some other toys.' Then she hastened to the sales counter.

I gave Charlie Chaplin one last yearning look and moved away.

On my birthday, Mum gave me a parcel tied with a pink ribbon. I untied the bow carefully. Inside was the Charlie Chaplin doll.

***

We left for the railway station early next morning. The place stank and the air was stifling. On the platform, flies settled on cow pats, and made them look like fruit cake. Men, women and children slept on the concrete floor, oblivious to the stench. Others hung out of carriages. Some even scrambled through the windows into the train.

'It's full!' I tried to shout loud enough to be heard above the noisy crowd. 'How can we go to Darjeeling?' I bit my lower lip.

'That's Third Class. We travel in a Second Class carriage. Dad has reserved our seats.' Mum's smile was reassuring.

After negotiating our way through the throng, we boarded a normal-sized train. Ever since our departure from Rangoon, Mum had been telling us we'd be travelling to the hills on a little train and I'd been looking forward to it. My shoulders drooped.

'We'll ride in the toy train as soon as we get to the foot of the mountain,' Mum said.

I slept for most of the time until we finally reached the tiny mountain-train. 'Let's go, Mum,' I cried, tugging at her hand.

I clambered on board, knelt on the seat and stuck my head out of the window. My heart thudded as the engine built up steam, then gave three toots before it pulled out of the station. I gazed at our train zigzagging its way up. How could a small engine pull so many carriages filled with people? My laughter bubbled up.

The higher we climbed, the more the thrills increased. Waterfalls cascaded down the mountain sides, and dwarf pines covered the slopes. Rhododendrons of various colours gave a splash of colour, but best of all was the sight of our little train straining up the mountain. Would we make it to the top?

***

At Darjeeling, after checking into our hotel, we set off for a walk. An old man limped towards us, leading three ponies.

'Are these for us, Daddy?' June asked.

'One for each of you,' he said.

I gazed wistfully as the man helped Rupert, Bertie and June mount the ponies. I longed to ride one too, especially the brown one with white socks, but I didn't dare ask. My chest ached, and I held back a sob.

A few minutes later, a boy hurried forward, dragging a little donkey by the reins. The donkey had red woollen tassels with chiming bells. To hold the rider in place, a brass circle several centimetres high surrounded the saddle.

'That's for you.' Mum lifted me off my feet and helped me into the seat.

I tipped back my head. The clouds passed and sunshine filled my soul.

A guide led us along treacherous tracks in the foothills of the Himalayas. I followed astride the donkey, guided by the old muleteer. Little thrills of pleasure ran up my spine as I stared down the steep sides of the mountain. The cool crisp air stirred my blood like an elixir.

We rode on until we came to a park. The horses halted, and the guides helped us dismount on the side of the road. June and I continued in an ecstasy of joy even after the ride, and spoke of our experience with cries of delight.

A horse galloped past and June spun round. 'That's Dad.'

I failed to recognise him as he shot by, but I'll never forget the pride in my sister's eyes as he disappeared in the distance.

***

The majestic snow-covered mountains whispered to me at nights as I snuggled down beneath the eiderdown, tired and happy.

One night, Rupert woke me, saying, 'Come and see this.'

'I'll call June,' I said.

'No. Dad will be angry if everyone gets up.'

Mystified, I followed him on tiptoe, rubbing sleep from my eyes. The moon had risen, leaving a silvery glow. Rupert stopped at a window facing the mountains, and pointed to an enormous bat perched on a nearby tree. It was eerie against the ghostly moonlight that immersed the snow-capped mountains in a shimmering light. My skin tingled and my heart beat fast. I pressed both palms to my cheeks.

I'd never seen a flying fox, but Rupert and Bertie had told us of blood-sucking vampires. I gazed at it from the safety of our room. I turned to Rupert and clasped my hands with joy because he'd chosen me to share the fascinating sight. A cameo captured and stored forever.

After drinking in the enchanting view, I crept to bed and fell back on my pillow. No amount of sorrow or suffering yet to come could erase the memory of the wonder and magic of that inimitable landscape. Darjeeling still beckons me to return and re-live that joyful moment.

***

The following year, Mum packed our clothes for another holiday. 'We'll be staying in a cottage by the sea.'

Mum had read us snippets from *Treasure Island*. My imagination conjured up thoughts of caves, pirates, smuggling, hidden gems and Long John Silver with his parrot. I visualised myself on the beach searching for jewels or building the world's largest sand castle.

On the way to the station, Bertie sang, 'We joined the navy to see the world and what did we see? We saw the sea.'

I clapped in time to the tune, and Rupert and June united their voices with Bertie. We were still singing when we boarded the train. It trundled along and we only stopped singing when we arrived at Moulmein and got into a cranky old bus that spluttered its way to our cottage at Amherst. 'Breathe in the fresh sea air and taste the salt,' Mum said as we alighted.

I licked my lips. They were salty, like blood.

The wooden holiday cottage was close to the beach, and rose about a third of a metre above the sandy soil. I longed to see the ocean, but it was already getting dark. After a meal of fish and chips, Mum sent us off to bed.

It was hours before I finally fell asleep. The excitement of anticipating all the joys of tomorrow kept me awake for a long time. The sob of the sea and the roar of the waves sounded in my ears as I drifted off to sleep.

***

Next morning, we walked to the beach. My toes tingled with the sandy grit creeping between them. A few bushes grew in patches and coconut palms waved in the breeze.

At my first sight of the sea, I searched for land on the other side. I stepped in gingerly and held my muscles rigid in fear of its immense emerald green depth and unending distance. I stayed close to the shore but a huge wave engulfed me.

Mum helped me up and everyone laughed—even Dad, who rarely joined in the fun with us.

Rupert and Bertie swam out to the breakers with Dad, and the waves carried them up. How brave they were!

Mum sat on the sand not far from me. 'You're sitting in the Indian Ocean,' she shouted above the sound of the waves.

'Are we in India?'

'India's over there.' She pointed further out. 'And far, far away is Australia, the land of kangaroos and koalas.'

I scanned the horizon but saw only sea.

June recited the poem Mum had taught us. 'Water, water everywhere, but not a drop to drink.'

Mum handed her a bottle of lemonade. 'Here's something to quench your thirst. Wait a bit and watch the sun go down to sleep.'

I raced out and grabbed a towel. Sitting on the sand, I waited. I held my breath as a red ball of fire slowly slipped into the sea and disappeared. 'Has it drowned? Is it dead? Will the sun ever rise again?'

'It wakes up in the morning just as you do.'

I could hardly wait to see the sunrise next morning.

***

That night, I awoke to the sound of voices in the living room.

'I was doing the rounds when I found Rupert's bed empty and the front door open,' Mum was saying.

'I'll ask the village headman to form a search party. Keep the children with you and get dressed.' Dad's voice sounded husky.

I rubbed my eyes and staggered out of bed. Bertie and June were already up. We changed into our day clothes and waited on the veranda. No one spoke. It was around one o'clock. The murmur of the waves and the ticking of the clock broke the silence. Time passed.

I must have fallen asleep. Bertie's voice woke me. 'They're here. They're here.'

'Pray. Pray that Rupert is safe,' Mum said.

Flashes of light pierced the darkness.

Not long after, Dad led Rupert in. He put his finger to his lips. 'We found him sleep-walking on the beach. Don't wake him.'

Mum reached for Rupert's other arm and my parents ushered him back to bed. While she tucked him in, Dad went to the bedroom for his wallet.

He returned with a note in his hand. I followed him and saw a huddle of dark faces in the dim light. They remained on the front steps and spilled out into the yard, waiting for payment.

'Your son was sleepwalking on the brink of the ocean. He must have heard the call of the sea.' The headman took the money, raised it to his lips and left with all the others.

After he'd gone, Dad said, 'The headman told me the outgoing tide could carry us out to sea. From now on we'll go swimming only when the tide is coming in.' He looked at Bertie. 'Neither you nor Rupert are to go into the water without me.'

***

That day, we walked to the colourful markets and bought fruit we'd never seen before—durians with thick green shells and long spikes, purple mangosteens and juicy watermelons. We watched Dad prise open a durian shell. An odour like a dead rat filled the room. We held our noses as he showed us the large cream-coloured pods inside, before handing one to each of us.

I waited until everyone else had taken a bite, then I licked the soft flesh, savouring it until nothing but the seed remained.

Mum couldn't bear the pong.

Next day, Dad bought some mangosteens. He crushed the purple fruit with the heel of his palms and exposed the snowy white pods. We loved the mangosteens. They didn't have a repugnant odour and even Mum enjoyed them.

In the afternoon, we wilted with the heat. Dad cut a watermelon into slices and the sweet, juicy fruit revived us.

I didn't realise it at the time, but they were teaching us geography through exotic fruit and learning about the sea.

***

The week before our holidays ended, I woke to hear Dad stomping around the cottage. The lights were on. I kicked off my blanket and slid out of bed, thinking that Rupert was out sleepwalking again.

'Bertie's not here. I'll search along the shoreline,' Dad said.

Mum stared at the open window in the boys' room. 'I shut it before going to bed. The front door is locked. He must have jumped out.'

'A noise awoke me. He may not have gone far.' Dad grabbed a torch and left.

Rupert, June and I rushed to the window. *Had Bertie fallen and broken a leg?* I bit my lip.

'It's not too high above the ground. I'm sure Bertie's not hurt,' June said.

On hearing her comment I walked unsteadily towards a chair and flopped down.

Mum paced up and down. 'Bertie must have answered the call of the sea. Ask God to keep him safe.'

My heart thudded. *Why did the sea call us?* Would I be next?

Rupert continually tapped his fist against his lips and stared at the floor. June sat quietly, her hands held together in prayer.

In less than half an hour, Dad returned. He had his arm on Bertie's shoulder and guided him towards his bed. Bertie had his eyes open, and he stared straight ahead.

'Thank God.' Mum helped tuck Bertie in. She took a seat beside Dad, her eyebrows raised.

Dad filled his pipe. 'I followed his footsteps in the sand and found him wandering on the beach.'

Mum turned to us. 'Go to bed, children. It's still too early to be up. The sun's not awake yet.'

I staggered back to the bedroom and threw myself down in my bed.

***

The day before we returned home, Dad went to the market and came back with a stack of durians. He laid old newspapers all along the bottom and sides of Mum's steel trunk and packed the fruit in.

'It'll stink and the stench will remain forever,' she moaned.

I crossed my arms, wondering what Dad would do. It was Mum's trunk, after all.

He took no notice of Mum's whingeing and continued to fill in the spaces between the fruit with newspapers, so they wouldn't roll against each other during the trip home.

For once, I sided with him. I was sorry for Mum—but I, too, loved durians.

Chapter 9

More Holidays

The past flows by like a stream, bringing to mind vivid memories of our trips to Kalaw, up in the mountains. I sat in the front, between Mum and Dad, but every so often I knelt on the seat and turned to talk to June in the back.

'Look at the lovely pine trees. Can you smell them?' June asked.

I bounced up and down on my knees and inhaled deeply. 'Yes. Oh, yes.'

Rupert gazed at the deep drop to the left of our car. Bertie gave an occasional glance at the steep precipice, but his eyes were riveted on Dad's hands as he shifted into lower gear and drove up the hill. Years later he told me he'd learned to drive by watching Dad, and didn't need any lessons before obtaining his licence.

The car strained up the slopes to the hill station.

'Something's burning,' Rupert said.

Mum sniffed and pointed to the engine. Blue flames shot out from beneath the dashboard, spewing heat on my face. Dad turned off the ignition and sprang out. Speechless, I clutched my arms and stared at the blaze.

Mum grabbed me and stumbled out of the car. 'Sand. Sand.'

We scooped up handfuls of soil and doused the motor until the fire was smothered. *How clever Mum was. She even knew all about cars!*

When the flames were quenched, Dad handed Rupert a bucket and told him to collect water from a waterfall back down around a bend in the road.

Rupert grabbed it and disappeared from sight. We waited. *Why was he taking so long? Had he been bitten by a snake or knocked over by another car?*

After several minutes Rupert returned. His shoes were wet and water splashed against the sides of the bucket at each step he took.

I watched the steam rise as Dad poured the cool liquid into the grumbling radiator. Then Rupert turned the crank handle while Dad pumped his foot on the accelerator to start the car.

In spite of such cantankerous behaviour, the old Austin served us until Herman was born, when it became too crowded and Dad bought the Chevrolet—a larger and grander vehicle.

I can never forget the time we drove up to Kalaw in our new car. It had been a hot summer and fires raged in the pine forests on either side of the road.

Mum's eyes widened but Dad refused to turn back. 'Only a forest fire.'

We forged ahead in a sea of smoke. The fire crackled and flames appeared to form an arc above our heads. I gasped for air. Tears stung my eyes. 'Who started the fire, Mummy?'

Mum wiped her eyes. 'When the wind blows the dry branches rub against each other and cause sparks.'

Glad that no one had been evil enough to start a fire and cause such devastation, I settled back and watched the fire. After a while, we passed blackened skeletons of trees and smouldering branches where the fire had already consumed itself.

Within an hour, we left the smoke far behind. The air cleared and once more the refreshing fragrance of pines saturated the atmosphere. The temperature dropped and little goose pimples appeared on my arms. Mum unzipped her carry bag and handed us our jumpers.

The shadows had lengthened by the time we arrived at Kalaw. The caretaker gave us the keys of a *dak*-bungalow and we settled in for the night. A *dak*-bungalow was a place where government officials could stay.

The following day, Dad took us for a walk while Herman remained behind with Nanny. On the way to the pine forests, he cut a branch off one of the cherry blossom trees lining the streets, and used it as a walking stick. Conifers covered the hills and formed a soft carpet of needles, emitting a sweet fragrance. Rupert and Bertie walked ahead with him. June and I stayed with Mum. At times, we stopped and collected some shiny brown cones. Whenever a raspberry bush reached out to us with its brambles, we picked the berries. Large and juicy, the pungent flavour remained in our mouths and the colour stained our hands.

Orchids with pendulous purple-and-white blooms grew on the topmost branches of the trees. 'Why can't Daddy get us an orchid?' I asked.

'Because he can't climb so high,' Mum answered.

My shoulders drooped.

Sometimes Dad took his gun along in the hope of spotting game. Once he shot a barking deer. Mum moved me away from the dead animal, lying limp in a pool of blood.

As I couldn't see the deer, Bertie described it for me. 'Soft brown fur and still warm.'

Rupert spared no detail. 'Dad shot it in the neck. Did you see it fall forward, kicking, eyes glazed and bloodshot? Its blood is all hot and sticky.'

June put her fingers to her ears and turned away.

'What'll we do with it, Mummy?' I asked.

'Daddy's going to the village to ask one of the villagers to skin it.'

I hopped up and down in excitement. I remembered a deer I'd seen at the zoo and imagined this standing beside the mantelpiece in our sitting room. 'Will they stuff the skin?'

'No. A taxidermist costs too much.'

'Will we have another pair of horns to hang our hats on?'

'The deer didn't have any antlers,' June said.

Mum placed her hand on my head. 'A barking deer's antlers are too tiny to use.'

That evening, a villager knocked at our door and brought us several cuts of venison. As Cook took his annual leave whenever we went on holidays, Nanny prepared our meals. She cut the meat into strips, then salted and hung them in the sun. When dry, she toasted it on an open fire. I sniffed. The appetising odour made me hungry.

Dad buttered a piece, took a bite of the crisp browned meat and smacked his lips. Mum smiled and held out her plate. My mouth watered.

My birthdays usually fell during our holidays but Mum gave me a present when we returned home. Dad bought me a packet of diamond-shaped *barafi*—an Indian sweetmeat made of milk, sugar and rose water. I'd cut the *barafi* into smaller diamonds and give a piece to everyone, then select a large one for myself and sink my teeth into the smooth white sweetmeat, letting my tongue caress my mouth until the cloying flavour no longer remained.

***

Our parents gave us pocket money every month, but they placed many restrictions on how we could spend it. Mum wouldn't let us buy anything from the stalls at school in case we caught diarrhoea, dysentery or typhoid. Dad refused to allow June or me to go to the movies with Rupert and Bertie.

On Fridays, he sometimes left work early and called in at school to take June to a matinee. He went to the secretary's office and requested approval to take June home before the bell rang. When her teacher received the message, June came to my classroom, and stood outside on the corridor.

I asked my teacher permission to talk to my sister, and rushed up to her.

'Daddy's outside. He's taking me to the pictures,' she said. 'I'm sorry you can't come.'

The corners of my mouth started to curl downwards. I wished Dad would take me along, at least once.

'Cook will pick you up,' June said.

When Cook came to take me home, I told him June had gone to the cinema. He carried my school satchel in silence, but held out his arm at right angles to his body, so I could swing on it like a monkey. At last I overcame my sadness and skipped home beside him.

***

Even as a child, I was a deep thinker. I did not speak much, but observed a great deal, watching the others, wondering and pondering. I had a dogged determination. Dad called it stubbornness but Mum said I was a persevering child, and praised me for studying hard.

She called Dad 'Mousie'. I never heard her call him Esau.

When I asked her why she'd given him that name, she shrugged.

'He creeps up behind me with his small, shifty eyes and peers around watching, watching.'

When I grew older, I often wondered how she could love him. I considered the nickname *Rat* more appropriate for him.

***

Our uncle, a Mathematics professor at Rangoon University, lived with his family at Pagan Hall, where he was rector. Every Sunday, we'd pile into our car to spend the day with our eight cousins. The drive through town took nearly an hour and I lounged back in the seat until we reached the countryside where whitewashed cottages overlooked terraced gardens with flowerbeds. Then I sat up and admired the view, knowing we were not far from the university.

About eighty students resided at Pagan Hall, one of the campus colleges. A tall man, always immaculately dressed, my uncle did everything with mathematical precision. He singled me out for attention because, whenever he met me, he posed an arithmetical problem for me to solve. He expected an answer at the conclusion of the day. I'd try to puzzle it out by myself and not ask help from anyone. Perhaps this accounted for my love of mathematics when I reached high school.

I recall riding in my cousins' blue toy car, pushing the pedals with my feet up and down the driveway until Mum called me in for lunch.

As the years passed, I joined Rupert, Bertie and our five male cousins, as they played *Hide and Seek* in the vast university grounds. The lawns were impeccable, the gardens constructed with paths bordered by rows of well-trimmed hedges and flowerbeds of carnations, phlox, snapdragons, cockscomb and other annuals. The buildings, lecture-rooms and students' quarters were out of bounds.

I always chose to shelter among the jasmine. The perfume of the flowers enchanted me as I tucked myself beneath a garden bench, or entwined my arms and legs around a pergola and clung to it.

My parents would sit and chat with Dad's sister. Uncle joined them for a cup of tea before excusing himself to continue work. My oldest cousin,

Tina, four years older than June, was too sedate to join us in the fun. She'd take my sister upstairs and show her all her trinkets and jewellery. Sometimes, she gave June a brooch or a trinket for keeping her company.

At times, they walked in the garden, pausing to inhale the perfume of the roses or admire a particular flower. Then I'd leave the boys and join them, as I loved the fragrances and vivid colours.

After lunch of *biriani*, a gastronomical delight of rice cooked in aromatic spices with chicken, we'd drive to the Kokine Lakes. It took less than ten minutes to get there. The water was warm and inviting.

I only ventured into the shallow part, dog paddling or floating on my back. Sometimes I swam out to Mum, who watched me in case I ran into difficulties. One day I called out and swam towards her, but she was playing ball and hadn't heard me. I found myself out of breath. I sank, gasping for air. I swallowed water. I didn't want to die. Overcome by fear, I splashed helplessly.

Suddenly, a pair of arms raised me out of the depths and took me to shallow water. I gulped in air and blinked. Dad stared down at me. By the time I regained enough breath to thank him, he had swum off. It was the closest to death I had ever been. Now, as an adult, I realise that God had saved me for a purpose.

***

One summer, our uncle hired a large bungalow at Thundaung, a hill station in the Shan States, and we went for a holiday with our cousins. Once we'd settled in, June and Tina teamed up as usual. But instead of gathering for a game as we usually did, Rupert and Bertie decided to go for a ramble in the forest. George, the eldest boy, who was three years younger than Bertie, joined my brothers.

Henry, who was the same age as me, chose to take me and explore an orchard near our bungalow. 'They'll probably scramble over rocks and get scratched by thorns.'

As we strode along, the soft summer breeze blew across the hills. We stopped at a strawberry patch and picked some fruit. Then seeing a guava tree laden with ripe yellow fruit, we gazed at them. Their odour drifted down to us and I imagined their sweet flavour in my mouth.

'Pick us,' they screamed.

I looked at Henry, urging him with my eyes.

He scrambled up the tree and gathered as many as we could carry. Then we hurried back, eager to share our spoils with the others.

On our way, we met the owner. He eyed the fruit. 'So you like guavas.'

'Yes.' The heat from a flush of shame mounted to my cheeks.

To my surprise, he was not annoyed with us for picking his fruit. Instead, he told us to return for more at three the next day.

The following afternoon when we knocked at his door, he greeted us with a bag full of guavas. There was sufficient fruit for everyone. I clasped my hands to my chest as we planned the next day's outing.

The next morning, I awoke to the sounds of quarrelling. My aunt screamed and pointed at a red mark on Henry's face. Mum stood by, biting her lip.

'All right. We'll leave.' Dad turned to Mum. 'Start packing our things straight away.'

My shoulders drooped. I'd been having so much fun.

Mum tossed our clothes into our cases and the boys carried them to the car. As we drove off I glanced back. No one stood on the verandah to wave goodbye.

'Why was Aunty angry?' I was surprised by their strange behaviour.

Mum leaned close to my ear. 'Henry annoyed Rupert while he was reading peacefully, so he lost his temper and struck him.'

Although only a year older than Bertie, Rupert was stronger than all the others put together, and none of us ever dared to anger him. *Why did Henry defy Rupert? Perhaps because his parents were around to protect him.*

I turned to the back seat. Rupert avoided my eyes. Maybe he thought I blamed him for having to leave Thundaung but I too would have been angry if anyone disturbed me while reading. I reached out and squeezed his shoulder.

Dad drove along the black ribbon of the Burma Road via the oil fields at Yenangaung. I dozed off, weary from watching the flat sandy plains.

A rushing, roaring sound wakened me. A raging river confronted us.

The rains had changed the area into a sea of muddy, swirling water and a torrent raced along, tearing trees up by their roots. A bridge spanned the small stream but the water had risen a few metres and covered it. We were trapped. *How could we get away?*

Dad stiffened. Then he backed the vehicle and made a detour on a minor road, bringing the car to a halt at a large sign warning us to beware of quicksands.

Mum clung to his arm. 'Please don't attempt the crossing. Think of the children. We'll be sucked under.'

I pictured us all drawn into the bowels of the earth and imagined the Chevrolet sinking deeper and deeper, until no light or air remained. *A coffin on four wheels!* Rupert and Bertie craned their heads to look at the floods but June compressed her lips.

Dad's eyes swept our surroundings.

A villager appeared on the road. He held a long bamboo pole in his right hand and had a bundle slung over his left shoulder.

Dad wound down the window and said something in Burmese. He must have requested him to lead us to the other side, because the man removed his bundle and waded into the water.

In the dim, dusky light, he walked ahead, using the pole to prod the riverbed.

The car roared as Dad turned on the ignition and drove into the torrent behind the man. Mum's cold hand gripped mine.

Our guide prodded the river bottom with his stick before stepping forward. He often changed course. Water swirled around the Chevrolet as Dad followed at a safe distance in low gear. On the far side, we emerged, dripping with mud. 'We couldn't have done it in the old Austin.' Dad fumbled for his wallet.

The villager held out his hand and my father placed a note in his open palm.

Dad switched on the headlamps, as darkness had fallen. Mum looked at the stream we'd just negotiated. 'What's the name of this place?'

'Pin Chaung. We're not far from the oil fields.'

She gazed ahead into the darkness. 'You know you suffer from night-blindness. Wouldn't it be safer to stop for the night and not try to press on?'

He shrugged. 'There's no hotel or *dak*-bungalow around.'

'If we're near the oilfields, Toungoo is just a few miles off. I've an aunt there. She'll be happy to put us up.'

'Let's try her then. She'll turn us away if we're not welcome.'

'Aunty will be glad to see me. I haven't seen her since we've been married.'

'Seems the only thing we can do.'

***

By the time we drew up at Aunt Abbie's house—a wooden structure raised on stilts—it was dark and moonless. The dwelling was huge.

'Look, Mummy,' I said, as the car's headlights flashed on the large garden filled with half a dozen or so fruit trees. 'They have lots of mangoes, but such tiny ones.'

'Those are marian plums,' Mum explained. 'If you're good, perhaps you may try some in the morning … but they're quite sour.'

Tired after so much driving, Dad left the engine running and stayed in the vehicle. His face was covered in sweat. He kept clenching his jaws and drumming his fingers on the steering wheel.

Mum got out and went to the front of the house. It remained dark and silent. No one came in response to her timid knocking. Dad gave a loud beep with the car horn.

After a few minutes, the door flew open and a young man stepped out. He appeared far bigger than Rupert. I couldn't hear Mum, but the youth, whom I later discovered was her cousin, went in to fetch his mother.

Aunt Abbie came out and kissed Mum. She strode to the car and shook hands with Dad before leading us inside. 'Leave your things here, and have a wash while I put something on the stove for you.'

By the time we had washed off the sweat and dust, dinner was ready. Aunt Abbie served us a hot meal and, after we'd finished, she escorted us back to what would be our room. She'd laid mattresses, blankets, pillows and bed linen on the well-polished floor while we were eating. She apologised for not being able to provide beds, and left us to settle down for the night.

The next morning, I awoke to find everyone at breakfast. I met our cousins—six young men in their teens. 'You have to wink when eating marians,' one said as he passed me a bowl of fruit.

They were sour. My eyes screwed up and I winked back at him.

Happy with my cousins and new surroundings, I soon forgot Henry and our hasty departure from Thandaung.

That was the only time I met them. Within a year, Toungoo was the scene of fighting between the Allies and Japanese forces—the town a blazing inferno, the wooden structures like blackened skeletons.

Did our cousins die during the bombing or on the trek to India?

It remains another of the war's unsolved mysteries.

***

A few months after our return, Mum had a baby girl whom she named Rose after her mother. Dad hired a new nanny to look after the baby and care for Herman, who was now too heavy for my old nanny to carry. Besides, she was no longer strong enough to manage him.

She had cared for each of us in turn, and Mum was sad to let her go. She walked with her to the door and waved as she left.

***

Our new nanny watched over Herman and Baby the whole day. After she had fed him his evening meal, she retired to the servants' quarters—a detached building behind the house, where she and Cook each had a room. Mum forbade us to enter the servants' quarters but in the evenings we often sat on the steps and watched Nanny as she prepared her makeup. A young unmarried village girl, her only qualification was the ability to speak English and look after us.

Nanny squatted on her haunches, placed some water on the surface of a flat circular stone and rubbed a small stick of sandalwood with a rotary movement. She continued this until a smooth, yellow liquid oozed into a groove and she smeared the stuff on her face. It dried in minutes, and left a pleasant perfume.

Nanny walked over to us. 'The bark keeps my complexion clear and fresh, and protects my skin from the ravages of the sun.'

'Do you have a boyfriend, Nanny?' June asked.

Nanny's eyes sparkled. 'Yes. He told me I was beautiful.'

She looked like an over-dressed puppet to me, but I recalled that Mum often said, 'Beauty is in the eye of the beholder.'

After one more glance in her mirror, dressed in all her finery, Nanny went out with her friend.

***

That December, Mum bought tickets for June and me to meet Santa, who lived deep within the British store affectionately known as Rowe's.

In the week leading up to Christmas, cool winter weather had replaced the hot, humid days. Filled with the magic and wonder of childhood, I squealed with delight as Dad drove us to the shopping area in the town centre.

Our car joined the bustling traffic in the tree-lined streets past Rangoon's Piccadilly Circus, the Sule Pagoda Road. Rangoon was in a festive mood. We passed brightly decorated department stores like Rowe & Co. and Whiteaways.

At Rowe's, a rainbow of intertwined lights lit their window displays. A large Christmas tree, laden with toys and artificial snow, stood dressed in finery befitting the most celebrated time of year. I grabbed Mum's arm and shook it, chuckling with delight.

People milled around, gazing in rapture at the decorations. The aroma of freshly baked bread from the Continental Bakery drifted into the open window. I eyed the selection of Christmas cakes displayed in the windows and longed for the one with Santa hauling a sack of gifts as he trudged in the snow-like icing. Leaning forward, I waited to see what Dad was about to do. I could hardly wait.

He entered the shop. Through the window, I saw him buy a Christmas cake and a dozen assorted little cakes. Dad returned to the car with three cardboard boxes. Carefully placing the large cake in the boot, he opened one of the boxes and selected a cake for himself. Mum was next to choose. I knew she'd take the chocolate-topped one.

Then it was Rupert's, Bertie and June's turn.

The wait was agonising. There were chocolate and coffee *éclairs*, sponge cakes with pink icing, or custard topped by a cherry in the centre and a cream-filled one that looked like a snail. I selected the snail.

'Lucky last,' Mum said.

I ate my favourite cake slowly, savouring every crumb. It oozed cream at each bite. I licked my lips, letting the sweet flavour remain in my mouth. The spun-out session lasted half an hour.

'Still eating, Hazel?' Dad drawled, and I nodded.

What a lucky girl I was. None of my friends drove in a Chevrolet or bought cakes from the Continental, Rangoon's top bakery.

How happy I was then, in total ignorance of the terrible times ahead.

Chapter 10

The Bamboo Telegraph

While we were at the refugee camp, I had frightful nightmares. I'd run from something or someone before finally falling into an abyss. These recurring dreams haunted me like a thief lying hidden in a subterranean cavern of my brain. The sounds of the jungle—the roar of a tiger or the scream of an ape breaking through the curtain of sleep—terrified me. I curled up, trembling beneath my blanket.

Those who had fled to the camp directly after the first bombing of Rangoon were able to provide themselves with some sort of comfort. Many had even brought radios, but discovered, to their dismay, the place had no electricity.

The delay at Katha had cost us most of our belongings. Dad bought a lamp, as candles were a hazard in the bamboo huts. To stretch out our dwindling savings, he purchased only the cheapest food.

I screwed up my face whenever I ate the local wild bananas. They had a centre of slimy seeds. Each mouthful stuck in my throat, refusing to go down. Mum couldn't eat them. They made her choke.

Under such conditions with such poor food, everyone had colds and runny noses. We ran out of handkerchiefs. Villagers would shut one nostril with a finger and blow out the snot, wiping their fingers on their *loongyis*. The sight of the mucus flying to the ground, leaving a green, slimy mess, revolted Mum. 'No wonder we all get colds. They spread their germs around.'

Before our evacuation from Rangoon, Dad had closely followed the events in Europe and the Far East. He'd stand with his head resting in his hand, his elbow propped on the sideboard, listening to the reports on the radio. Sometimes, half-hidden in his easy chair, he'd scour the papers for an update of the fighting.

Government officials censored the information in an effort to maintain morale. The broadcast invariably commenced: 'Do not listen to rumours. Here is the news.'

Now, deprived of our radio, only rumours filtered through. Our lives and fortune hung in a balance and news of the war meant everything. The most obscure and incidental piece of gossip was as priceless as a pearl.

On crowded station platforms, rigid rules of etiquette and pride of birth gave way to fear and the insatiable desire for facts and figures. Trains hissed into northern Burma laden with refugees who brought stories of conditions down south. People spoke to acquaintances, railway staff and strangers. They shouted out inquiries about friends and relatives, asking for the latest news on the fighting.

***

Meanwhile, Japanese troops swept northwards and Toungoo fell by mid-March. In 1942, Mum's younger brother, Pat Scriven, who worked as a guard in the railways, helped evacuate the wounded by train. When the British left town after town, railway employees remained behind. Pat continued to carry out his duties until senior officials of the Burma Railways ordered all staff to leave.

We met Uncle Pat several years later. He'd been in Pyinmana, about four hundred kilometres north of Rangoon, when the Japanese bombed the town. He had tried to join his brother George, but finding the roads cut, he tossed in his luck with a work-mate, Fred.

They boarded a military hospital train bound for Maymyo, a sleepy railhead only forty kilometres east of Mandalay, then a frontier town born from the hostilities. Loaded with wounded soldiers from the front line, the train disgorged casualties at Maymyo station. Even after the wounded had been taken to hospital, the carriages still smelled of rotting flesh. Flies hovered around bloodstains.

The train proceeded to a refugee camp in Kyetta, a village twenty kilometres further on. Fred and his wife went there because their children were too young to trudge through unmapped and inhospitable jungle. Pat remained with them.

When the Japanese arrived, they confiscated most of the provisions the British had provided the refugees.

'To earn something for food, Fred and I formed a band and entertained people, scraping together a few rupees,' Pat told us years later.

An undercover agent for the Allies, disguised as a monk, sometimes sent a bunch of bananas from the monastery. In desperation, Fred, realising they'd all perish if things didn't improve, offered his two eldest sons into the agent's safekeeping.

The monks accepted the boys as young disciples and they remained at the monastery for the duration of the war. They survived without mishap, gaining a sound knowledge of the Burmese language and culture while retaining their Catholic faith.

Within a few months, Japanese military police, suspecting underground activity in the area, dragged Fred away for interrogation. Pat, nearly dying of cerebral malaria at the time, escaped questioning. Medicine was unavailable, but Fred's wife fed him small chunks of raw liver each day. My uncle awoke from his delirium, and lived to support the family until his friend's return.

After Fred's release, whenever Lancasters rained bombs near them, he would sing *Rule Britannia* at the top of his voice and wave to the RAF planes until friends dragged him into a trench. The interrogation by Japanese police only served to increase his loyalty to the British.

No matter how difficult or dangerous the circumstances, Uncle Pat kept everyone amused with his jokes. He took to drink due to the stress, and couldn't break the habit when peace returned.

At the end of hostilities, his brother George, with the help of a new wonder drug, succeeded in curing him of his love for the bottle.

Years later at our meeting with Pat, he explained. 'The medication causes projectile vomiting whenever I consume the slightest amount of alcohol. The vomit is rainbow-coloured and makes me feel quite ill. It's an effective cure.'

***

Refugees brought us news of an incident at Thaton, further south. An Anglo-Indian friend, Steve, who worked as a guard, boarded a train carrying equipment and food for the frontline. When he arrived, the station was deserted. The engine driver, fearing the town was already in enemy hands, fled into the jungle.

Two British soldiers sat smoking on the platform. The concrete around them was littered with cigarette butts and their uniforms were stained.

'Where are the other soldiers?' Steve asked.

'Evacuated,' someone replied.

Steve's eyebrows shot up. 'Then why haven't you left?'

'We were detailed to empty some water tanks at a temple and have just got back.' He stopped and glanced around. 'The Japs haven't arrived yet. They think our men are still here.'

'You're damn lucky they do. We'd better get out now.'

The other soldier threw down his cigarette and extinguished it with the heel of his boot. 'How the hell can we do that without any transport?'

'I've worked in the British Railways,' the other said. 'I'll drive if you fellows stoke the boilers.'

Refugees clambered on board when they saw the men preparing for departure. Ten minutes later the train steamed off with passengers hanging onto any available hold.

This is just one example of the confusion that reigned in the railways during the retreat from Burma. Back in the jungle, however, we knew nothing of the wider picture.

***

Mandalay, the second largest town in Burma, stood deep in the dry belt in the country's heartland. Early in 1942, the sleepy town awoke to the grim realities of war. The bamboo telegraph brought news of sick and wounded soldiers arriving daily from the frontline. Trains were over-crowded with the casualties; wounds turned septic for lack of medical aid.

To prevent congestion and the spread of disease, the government held refugees in a transit camp ten kilometres outside Mandalay. Here cholera, dysentery and smallpox broke out, making life a sea of suffering. By the beginning of April, hospitals became so congested casualties awaited treatment in the corridors.

On 4 April, waves of Japanese bombers pounded the city for three hours, killing three thousand and injuring another five thousand. Fifth Columnists lit fires, directing aircraft to their targets. Arsonists cut fire hoses and set ablaze the southern suburbs where administrative offices, police barracks, houses of civil and railway officers, and European businessmen lay.

The home where Rupert, Bertie, June and I were born was one that burned down.

Ammunition and oil tankers exploded, water mains burst and the electricity powerhouse shuddered to a stop. People ran up and down the streets, their faces contorted by fear. The railway station remained unserviceable during the retreat—all trains had to terminate at Myohaung, further south.

Refugees fled through the Kawbaw Valley and over the hills, trying to reach the safety of India. Others escaped to Myitkyina, about five hundred kilometres north, where it was rumoured it was possible to fly out of the war zone to India.

On 27 April 1942, railway staff left Maymyo for Myitkyina. They stocked the train with rice, sugar, Ovaltine and condensed milk, and steamed away. As the engine driver stopped whenever water was available, the normally two-day journey lasted a whole week. Food stalls were no longer open for business, so he also halted at nights for passengers to gather firewood to cook their meals.

The train limped into Myitkyina on 4 May, too late for anyone to obtain a flight into India. Some decided to find shelter and hope their provisions would see them through the war. Others joined in the great trek across the Himalayas.

By the end of April, the three generals Slim, Alexander and Stilwell decided to leave Burma before it was too late. They ordered British and Indian troops to retreat over the Ava Bridge to the western side of the Irrawaddy. The following day, British sappers blew up the bridge.

The Allies set up new Headquarters at Shwebo, 110 kilometres north on the Mandalay-Myitkyina railway line. A regiment of the Chinese 38th Division took over control of the garrison at Mandalay, while their 22nd and 96th Divisions withdrew to the north-east to protect China's frontier.

After the withdrawal of the British from Mandalay, anarchy reigned. At nights, Burmese assaulted Chinese soldiers whenever they went out in search of food. Forced to shelter within the fort, the military only ventured out in the daytime to shoot looters and arsonists.

When Japanese planes bombed the city once more, the Chinese 38th Division retreated. Mandalay fell on 30 April, two days after my eighth birthday.

Chapter 11

Nightmare Trails and Terrible Tales

When we were at Katha, Dad met up with a man called Mr Singh and invited him over to the camp. Mr Singh, an agent of the Irrawaddy Flotilla Company, had been in Mandalay during the bombing. Dad had first met him when accompanying a High Court judge on his tours in pre-war days.

They squatted on the bamboo floor of our hut. Rupert and Bertie sat on the steps. Mum made tea, while June carried Rose. I brought out two enamel mugs filled with the hot brew. Returning to the living room, I eavesdropped on their conversation. Nanny, feeding Herman his broth, beckoned me to come away. I took no notice.

'How are things at Mandalay?' Dad filled his pipe. When we fled Rangoon he had packed sufficient tobacco for six months, thinking the Allies would return as soon as the monsoons passed.

Singh did not mince words. 'What a damn mess it has been! Only towards the end of April did authorities order hospital staff to evacuate patients to Myitkyina.' His voice rose to a higher pitch. 'There was only room for the staff and patients. Doctors escorted the wounded from Mandalay by train, and casualties from Prome went up the Irrawaddy by steamer.' His voice rose another couple of scales. 'Some were transferred to Katha. At Myitkyina, nurses found the airstrip cluttered with stretcher-cases waiting to be flown out to India. Priority was given to the sick and wounded, so most of the refugees couldn't board a plane and had to trek out.'

'How's the governor?'

'Sir Reginald joined General Hutton, who had set up Headquarters at the University.'

My mind flashed back to the fun we'd had with our cousins there. I imagined soldiers swarming all over, trampling on the flowerbeds and horses dragging the gun carriages into the grounds. How I longed for a handful of flowers!

I peered through a slit in the bamboo matting.

'Was that the last stronghold in Rangoon?' Dad asked.

Singh's face remained grim. 'More like a final rallying point. The governor stayed at military headquarters as long as he could. In the end, he flew out with General Hutton to meet Wavell. Sir Reginald wanted to trek out, but Churchill sent a message ordering him to get out at once.'

Dad looked long and hard at Singh. 'And so he should. I hope he succeeded.'

'Just made it. Flew out from Myitkyina at dawn on the 5th of May. Japs raided the airport, but the RAF left with the governor and the wounded, before the air-strip was overrun.'

'Has the town fallen to the Japs?'

'My dear chap, its fate was inevitable. The main body of Chinese fought in the Shan States to protect their own borders. When Lashio, the last outpost on the eastern frontier, fell, Myitkyina was evacuated. Japs were within nineteen miles of the town by then.' He paused, letting the enormity of his words sink in.

My breathing came in short gasps. I hoped my father wouldn't hear me through the mat walls.

Dad pressed on after a brief silence. 'What about the civilians?'

'Those capable of walking commenced the trek through the Hukawang Valley and over the Naga hills to India. Others stayed in the care of priests and nuns who intend to remain on with their flock. The Columbans had been asked to take over the Bhamo Civil Hospital. It's less than a hundred miles south of Myitkyina, you know. Mandalay, Bhamo and Myitkyina fell like dominoes.' Singh took a deep breath.

'Why are you still here? Shouldn't you leave when you can?'

'I'm an Indian national. I'll pretend to be a Chandra Bose sympathiser, so the Japs won't harm me.' Singh drew himself up to his full impressive height.

We'd heard of Chandra Bose, an Indian nationalist and leader of the left wing of the Congress Party, who'd recruited Indian volunteers to fight for the enemy. *What a traitor!*

'I've been helping with the evacuation,' Singh continued. 'Only yesterday I obtained transport for a detachment of Burma Frontier Force and their Scottish officer.'

'I saw them crossing the river,' Rupert piped up.

My eyes widened as I leaned forward to catch every word.

Singh heaved a sigh. 'I hope they manage to elude the Japs and get to India before the monsoons.'

He paused, gazing into the distance. 'In 1941, Chinese troops arrived here singing and laughing, confident of being able to defeat the Japanese. Now they are hunted down by both Burmese and Japanese. Because they'd lived off the land like locusts and raided their crops, the Burmese capture solitary Chinese soldiers and bury them alive.'

He extended his hand and hurried off after a quick handshake.

***

In the first week of May 1942, Myitkyina fell into chaos. A seething mass of humanity swelled refugee camps within the city. At the airport, DC 7 Dakotas manned by the American Volunteer Group flew out women and children to India. Despite constant air attacks, they loaded planes to capacity and returned repeatedly until just before the town fell to Japanese forces.

Local boys drove busloads of evacuees to the aerodrome. Tommy, one of the volunteers, dropped off a busload, then waited on the tarmac to wave goodbye to his family. The pilot recognised him and offered him the last seat on the plane. Tommy did not hesitate to buckle himself in.

Those left behind tried storm the plane before it took off, but they were forced to watch as it lumbered into the air, leaving them behind. They had no choice but to risk the hazardous trek across the Naga Hills to India.

Only local hill tribes and timbermen of the Bombay Burma Corporation, who travelled on elephants during the dry season, had previously used the trails. No proper maps of the area were available. Refugees had to climb the Himalayas and trek via the Hukawng Valley. It came to be called the Valley of Death. During those terrible times, thousands congested the tracks.

City dwellers mingled with military personnel who had remained behind to carry out demolition work. First the trekkers waded through muddy swamps, then trudged in dense jungle until finally reaching the lofty mountains.

In one group, a solitary figure rode an elephant with his rations, rifle, bedding and umbrella strapped to its back. A lone woman carried a bamboo pole on her shoulders with a bucket at each end. One held her worldly possessions. The other, bouncing along in rhythm with her weary steps, contained her baby. Others staggered on in a trance.

Along the way, corpses lay in various states of decay, fouling the air and attracting myriads of flies. Monkeys swung beside them, shouting and screaming at each other. The muddy tracks showed footprints of tigers and leopards. During the night lone travellers were dragged off as prey.

***

The American general, Stilwell, commanding the Chinese forces in Burma, placed his Army in a rear-guard position on both sides of the Irrawaddy. Trekking out via the Hukawang Valley, he started out with eighty in his party. British, Indian and Chinese refugees swelled the number as he progressed.

Villagers worked in relays, lugging food and clothing for his party. Naga tribesmen were invaluable as guides. They carried the sick on stretchers, and toted Stilwell's tommy-gun whenever he let them.

The general paid them in gold or silver coins and reached India without any loss of personnel. When the monsoons arrived, however, rivers became impassable. Those who commenced the trek after him fell victim to disease and starvation.

***

Some fifty years later, I met Larry, who had walked out about the same time as Stilwell. His story is one of the few with a successful conclusion.

Larry worked as a foreman in Namtu refineries. He had married in September 1941. Early in May 1942, when he joined the army at Namtu, his wife Dolores was six months' pregnant. His wife and sister tried to catch a plane at Lashio but, owing to the congestion on roads, they arrived too late.

Once back at Namtu, the British officer in charge of troop evacuation told the two women to board a vehicle bound for Myitkyina. There the AVG were still ferrying refugees by air. The truck contained silver bars but, as instructions were issued to only fly military personnel, the driver dumped his freight into the river.

He turned to Dolores. 'Sorry, Madam, orders are orders. I'm afraid you'll have to make your own way to India.'

Dolores and her sister had no alternative but the Hukawng Valley. Death lurked in the wings but they stayed alive by rifling the pockets of corpses for food. Many times Dolores wanted to slip away from the others and lie down to die, but the thought of her unborn infant kept her going. The baby in her womb sapped her strength. Still she struggled on.

While Dolores and her sister were trekking to India, Larry and five members of the Burma Auxiliary Force hitched a lift on a truck to Bhamo, further north. There the British demolition team destroyed banknotes, distributed silver coins to Larry and his companions, and ordered them to leave for India.

The army had scuttled hundreds of ships from the Irrawaddy Flotilla Company and many lay askew in the river. Larry boarded an abandoned ship and helped himself to lentils, rice, Bovril, Marmite, cigarettes, tea, sugar, tins of cocoa, water bottles, a large kerosene oil tin for cooking, and a kettle.

After distributing the provisions among his group, he commenced the trek armed with a 12-bore shotgun and a .45 revolver. Not long after, he stopped to question two soldiers sitting by the side of the track.

'We're the only survivors of a Japanese attack,' one replied. 'He's from the Cameroon Division, and I'm from the Inniskilling Division. Our entire companies have been wiped out.'

Larry invited the men to join him, filled two knapsacks with rice for the journey and handed one to each of them. They commenced walking at four am, trekking about fifty kilometrea each day. Whenever they passed trees laden with green mangoes, Larry shot the fruit down to complement their daily food ration. He ordered a halt for lunch at mid-day, and camped for the night around four pm. Whenever possible, he bivouacked near a stream of fresh water. After a refreshing swim, the men cooked their evening meal of rice, lentils, Bovril and birds they shot along the way.

'It was fun,' Larry said, before continuing on a more serious note. 'One day, the youngest man, a mere boy, told me he couldn't go on. I reached for the kettle, shared the water around, lit a fire to smoke out the mosquitoes, and left the party. Taking the fittest man along, I went in search of a stream. We stumbled about in the dark, but after a while, we discovered a pond and brought back enough water for cocoa.

'The next morning, the youth was much better and we resumed the trek. I realised we had filled our containers from a dank, green pool. As it was fetid, we re-filled our bottles at the first stream we passed.

'Sometime after, we met Nagas who were travelling in the same direction and hired them to carry our knapsacks to the top. They picked up our kit, threw them across their shoulders and loped uphill, leaving us far behind. Thinking the tribesmen had taken off with our packs, we trudged despondently up the crest. To our surprise, the Nagas had arranged the gear in a row before leaving.'

Larry called a halt and ordered each man to collect his pack. While resting, he poured his silver coins out on a ground sheet and put them in piles for counting.

A twig snapped and a half-naked Naga appeared, gazed at the money and raced off, shouting and waving his spear. Within a few minutes, the tribesman and his companions returned. Each warrior held a wad of notes and indicated they wanted the coins for use as ornaments. Delighted, Larry and his men exchanged the heavy coins for the lighter and more valuable paper money.

A week later, the group caught up with retreating Allied troops.

Larry joined them and took out a packet of cigarettes to smoke, during a halt.

No sooner had the smell of tobacco reached the soldiers than a tall blond private strode towards him. He laid an enamel mug of steaming hot water and a shaving stick on the grass. Then he produced a pair of hair clippers from his knapsack and glanced at Larry's unkempt hair.

'Would you like a haircut in exchange for a few cigarettes?'

Larry agreed to the bargain, and enjoyed the luxury of a hairdresser in the dense Burmese jungle.

When they arrived after a trek of nearly three weeks, Imphal had just been raided and smoke curled skywards from the town. Larry's shoulders sagged at the sight of burned and bombed buildings. He had looked forward to a hot bath or at least a basin of warm water to soak his sore and blistered feet. Now he had nowhere to rest.

As he trudged in the rubble-strewn streets, two military police officers stopped him. 'The town was bombed yesterday, but we have bread and sausages for you lot.'

One jerked his head towards a distant tent. 'Just hand over the weapons and follow your nose. They'll provide you with a meal and a mug of hot tea.'

Before leaving to join their own Companies, the two British soldiers who had accompanied Larry during the trek embraced each of the men in turn.

After Larry had satisfied his appetite, he was sent by truck to a refugee camp not far from Dimapur. The officer-in-charge gave him a long, thick bamboo cane and ordered him to supervise the evacuation of newly arrived refugees.

Larry threw his shoulders back and thrust his chest out, ordering the pushing, shoving refugees to stand back. Their impetus continued until he swung his cane, threatening them.

When the refugees had all boarded the trucks, Larry dropped down on the floor of the lorry and drew up his knees. The odour of unwashed bodies filled the truck, and his muscles cried out with each bump in the road. He shut his eyes and, tapping his foot, thought of Dolores. *Was she safe? When would he see her again?*

On reaching Dimapur, Larry met his father and sister. They had flown out with the AVG. He searched all the bulletin boards and made inquiries for his wife but no one could give him any information.

At first, the military sent him to Ranchi, then to Dimapur, finally posting him to Mahow at the Elephant Barracks. There he received equal wages and privileges as British ordinary ranks.

He was eventually transferred to the Malcolm Barracks and given three months' leave. Soon after, a telegram arrived informing him Dolores was in Calcutta. Throwing his arms up into the air like a marathon winner, he raced to his Colonel, obtained permission to go to Calcutta, and received a railway pass.

He pushed his way through the crowded station and boarded the train. As it chugged along, he prayed his wife would be well enough to undergo the trauma of childbirth in her weakened condition.

He arrived in time for the premature birth of his son, Maxwell. The baby survived the long trek of twenty-nine days, although stricken with malaria while still in his mother's womb.

***

One particular incident wrenched my heart when I heard of it. The headmistress of Bishop Strachan Home for Girls commenced the walkout with several of her staff and thirty-six Anglo-Burmese girls. The youngsters shivered with cold in their thin white cotton uniforms. The rains came, food ran out, many fell ill. Still they trudged up slippery slopes, existing on a cup of hot tea for breakfast and some rice at the end of the day's trek. One by one, they collapsed from hunger and weariness. The official-in-charge finally decided to go ahead and get food for them. He reached a British outpost and hurried back with food, but collapsed and died before reaching them.

Four of the group reached India, but two died within a few days.

In another group, a young girl suffered an intense itch on her head. She screamed and tore at her hair. Friends discovered a nest of maggots on her scalp.

The pests bored into her brain, driving her insane. The friends abandoned her, as all were in survival mode.

Many trekkers died from cholera or exhaustion. *Dacoits* waited in the shadows to rob them. Blood gushed from the gaping wounds of their victims who held out their hands, pleading for aid. Refugees passed by them, unable to offer any help. Delay meant certain death.

Parents urged dying children to get up and walk. Rain fell incessantly. Within ten days, the incubation period of malaria, many refugees dropped by the wayside. No one escaped the bites of myriads of mosquitoes, leeches, huge dum-dum flies and tiny buffalo flies.

Millions of leeches, ranging in size from two to ten centimetres, marched ominously out of the jungle. They stretched forward, heads touching tails and forming a hump. Hideous and stealthy, they clung to victims, swelling from pin-sized to the thickness of a finger thirty centimetres in length.

At first, the bites initiated a slight itch all but lost among countless bruises. The bites itched for days, and later formed an ulcer and consumed the flesh, exposing the bone.

Trekkers removed leeches with salt or petrol, or burned them off with lighted cigarettes. Leeches writhed and exploded on the decomposed litter underfoot when touched with a red ember or cigarette. Still victims continued to endure a sensation of crawling and sucking. The toxins accumulated, each bite causing more itch, until the mere sight of one filled sufferers with fear and loathing.

Over half a century later in the Australian bush, a leech bit me in my mouth, bringing home some of the hardships the trekkers must have experienced. I had slipped and as I wiped the soil off my face, the slippery slimy creature entered my mouth.

In panic, I jumped up and down.

My husband was able to dislodge it with salt, but the crawling sensation remained for the rest of the day and lingered on for weeks.

***

Donald Mellican was a member of the Territorial Army during the time of invasion. He left his three brothers and two sisters to enrol in the regular army when Britain called for volunteers.

Donald's father, Arthur Mellican, an engineer in the south of Burma, assisted in Britain's scorched earth policy before the enemy arrived. He fled north, knowing he would be imprisoned and tortured, if he remained.

At Myitkyina, Donald arranged for his family to join the trek via the Hukawng Valley to India. Then he left to fight with his unit against the advancing Japanese. Desperate from lack of provisions and fresh water, he searched the pockets of corpses for food.

Despite malaria and starvation, he reached India four weeks later. Doctors sent him to hospital and, on his discharge, the military granted him leave to search for his family. He immediately left for Calcutta, hoping to glean some news of them. Twice a day he visited the Loretta Convent, where the nuns provided food and shelter for evacuees from Burma.

He pinned a message on the notice board, hoping for information, to no avail.

On expiry of his leave, Donald was drafted into the new intelligence unit to work behind enemy lines in Burma. In 1943, he continued his search, and sent letters to the Gurkha Embassy, the Salvation Army and the Red Cross. Once again success dodged him.

He is still searching for them.

Donald's story is one of the many stories of people torn apart from their families by war and left in ignorance of their fate. It could well have been our family's tale if we, too, had trekked out.

***

As the years turned to decades, we met many others with similar stories. After the war, my brother, Bertie, worked as the principal of a missionary school in Myitkyina. There he heard reports from Burma's extreme north—where India, China and Tibet meet in a triangle.

In early 1942, people arrived at the mission on their way to India. Colonel Stevenson handed over forty-nine refugees to two Irish Catholic priests and left provisions for them. The priests departed to arrange transportation but, during their absence, Chinese troops stole all their food. By the time the priests returned with transport, the monsoons had broken and rivers were impassable.

When the rains ceased in October, the clerics led the refugees to Fort

Hertz in the foothills of the Himalayas. From there, a plane flew them out to India for rest and recuperation. At that time the fort was the only territory within Burma not yet taken by the enemy.

The military granted the priests free board and lodging for the duration of hostilities. However they insisted on returning. Detachment 101, a unit of the Office of Strategic Services, dropped them back to their beloved Kachins in northern Burma. The two chaplains led their parishioners in guerrilla warfare, harassing the Japanese. At the time, I did not know that Mum's brother, George, had also joined the underground forces and was known as 'the Fighting Padre'.

Chapter 12

Marooned by Monsoons

One day at the refugee camp in Kyuktongyi stands out in my mind. Two girls whose family had also evacuated from Rangoon handed their skipping rope to June and me, then jumped in and told us to swing the ropes faster and faster. When our turn came, we couldn't skip even half as long.

We rested and nattered on until June rose to her feet. 'Mum's all alone. We'd better go back now.'

On our return, Mum threw up her hands. 'The hut is so small. The walls seem to be caving in and about to crush us.' She glanced at the door. 'I wonder where Dad is.'

I slumped down on the floor. *How could I help Mum? Why did Dad stay away for so long? What was he doing?* I guessed my brothers would be out exploring the jungle. They loved adventure.

Baby cried and Mum offered her breast to her. She drank greedily. June hovered over them like a ministering angel. I gnawed on my lower lip.

The sun was low on the horizon when Mum finally said, 'Perhaps he's visiting a friend at one of the huts. The boys are not back from their walk. June, stay with me. Hazel, go and find your father.'

Always willing for adventure, I trudged off. Dad often visited other huts to glean news of the war. I stood outside each dwelling, straining my ears for his voice. The wind blew, sending up clouds of dust.

Dusk spread its dark cloak and I knew I didn't have much time. I continued searching until, turning the corner to look in the second row of huts, I saw a group of men in a circle. They were speaking in hushed voices.

Something terrible must have happened.

I edged closer to listen. Then I glimpsed Dad among them. I'd not seen him at first because of his short stature.

'The Japs have four divisions,' Mr Rees said. 'One has moved via the oilfields, another up the Rangoon Mandalay trunk road. The third is advancing into the Shan States towards China. The fourth is staying put.' He must have known so much because his brother served in Mandalay as a young officer in the British army.

Mr Rees paused and swatted a fly bathing in the perspiration on his brow. His face was red with sunburn. 'The Allies have no fresh troops and are exhausted. The government has recalled the RAF to India and we're without air support. I'll join my sister at Myitkyina and fly out.'

'We'll trek to India.' Mr D'Cruz's face perspired profusely and his mouth was pinched. 'The planes are only taking women and children.'

A short silence followed. I pictured the overweight figure of Mr D'Cruz staggering along, his wife struggling behind. I visualised them laden with sacks tied to their backs, climbing the steep hills of the Himalayas. In my mind's eye, the track had a sheer drop on one side like the one in Darjeeling.

'The mountains are nineteen thousand feet high. Not a Sunday afternoon stroll, you know.' *Was there venom in Dad's voice as he spoke?* Mr D'Cruz was a colleague Dad had long considered stood in his way to promotion.

'The Chinese were expected to hold eastern Burma, but they too are retreating,' another man said hastily. *Perhaps he was trying to avert an argument.* 'The Japs will be here any day. I'll remain behind until the war is over. I've a daughter about the same age as yours.' He looked at me.

Dad glanced in the direction of his gaze. 'What are you doing here?' His voice sounded like the crack of thunder. 'Get back to the hut immediately.'

I grew cold. My breathing turned shallow in an instant. I swung around and ran, suppressing my sobs. *My father had shouted at me before his friends!* Humiliated and blinded by tears, I found my way back to our hut and stumbled up the steps to Mum.

'What's wrong, Hazel? What happened?'

'Dad yelled at me and sent me back.'

Mum held me in her arms until I quietened down. Then she served us our dinner and tucked me into bed with June.

The next day, Mum explained the news Dad had just heard—news of the retreat by the Allies—had caused him to explode. 'Besides, the humid weather just before the monsoons makes one irritable.'

I never forgot that incident, and despite Mum's explanation, I couldn't forgive him for his harsh words to me in public.

***

Soon after our arrival in the village, a change came over the jungle. The nights were breathless with occasional dust storms. Black clouds thickened, building up and up on each other's backs. The heat and humidity oppressed us. Then a rumble resonated across the mountains. Coming ever closer, it exploded like thousands of bombs, shattering the stillness and rolling from one end of the horizon to the other. Lightning illuminated the hut and threw an incandescent glow from the thatched roof to the darkest corner of the room.

Amid the explosion of thunder, the hissing and thrashing of leaves sounded like an express train. I trembled in fear and ran to Mum. She put an arm around me and drew me close.

Rain splattered on the dust, sending it flying as if a meteorite had crashed. One drop followed another until it fell in sheets, sweeping all before it. Puddles formed, turning to ponds and lakes. The land changed into an earth-brown porridge, leaving a slippery, slushy surface. Rivers overflowed their banks.

People caught out in the full fury clung to trees, but the winds often swept them away. Roads, often no more than dirt ruts, turned to rivers of mud. Our hut was marooned.

The monsoons had arrived.

***

Our stopover at the village stretched like an elastic band. Months passed. Even June lost her cheerfulness. An invisible thread connected me to her.

Her vivid imagination conjured visions of burning houses and people with feet torn from walking on thorn-covered twigs scattered on the hot ground. Like my own fearsome thoughts.

At nights, I dreamed of the past, our wonderful days at Rangoon, our home, our holidays, and my dolls. At Rangoon, I loved hearing storms growling from the security of my home. I used to look out the window at masses of clouds shutting out the heavens until an insistent rain blurred the windowpanes. The trees had been silent in a misty, melancholic reverie. Not like this.

During our first few days at the village, Bertie had told jokes and played on his mouth organ. I was breathless with excitement during the picnics in the jungle. Life was still an adventure when gathering wild flowers in the days before the monsoons. Now it remained wet, soggy and muddy. Rain thrashed all around, falling obliquely into the bamboo huts. A grey-green fungus began to grow everywhere.

The village had no public services, running water or sanitation. Confined in the refugee camp, frustration took its toll and tempers flared. Dad's disposition became intolerable. Unable to go outdoors, we moped around with nothing to do. June no longer played imaginary games with me.

Other children had brought their toys, but I didn't possess a single doll; Rupert and June had no books to read. Bertie had his mouth organ but I seldom heard him play it. *If only Mum had let me bring Toddles!*

***

One night, June shook me awake from a deep sleep. 'You've taken *the entire* blanket.'

I was in a warm cocoon, and remained still, too sleepy to move.

June hit me. I responded by hitting her and rolling over. Mum knocked on the mat partition between our rooms and told us to settle down.

I fell back and slept.

The next morning both of us had forgotten all about the incident, but in later years I would mull over it. Perhaps the cold and hunger had caused us to turn against each other that night, driving us to fight for the blanket.

***

The Allies continued their fighting retreat. When Slim's troops reached the Chindwin just north of Kalewa, an ambush awaited them. A storm of bullets poured down from the cliffs. The men fired back before crossing the river in barges with their wounded.

Outnumbered, out-armed and outflanked, dark clouds of defeat rolled over the army. As they neared the border, British tea planters met them, transporting as many as possible to Tamu, the village on the boundary between India and Burma. From there, a Liaison Officer sent casualties by lorry to Imphal and Kohima in Assam. The rest straggled on towards India.

The rearguard was still eighty kilometres from India when the monsoons began. For the last ten days of the retreat, the heavens wept floods of tears on the tired troops. Visibility was less than two metres, the rain cold and hard like pellets of ice.

At the site of the ambush at Kalewa, the rear-guard passed bloating corpses, expended shells and abandoned equipment. The Japanese were no longer there.

They had fled back to Burma when the monsoons broke.

Twelve thousand Allied troops arrived at Imphal, the capital of Assam, after squelching through swamps. The longest fighting retreat in British history.

The isolated garrison on the north-east frontier never imagined war would ever encroach on their territory. Officers led a luxurious life-style and indulged in a whirl of social activities.

When the civilian evacuees arrived, government officials transported them to cities in India. Military personnel housed the influx of exhausted soldiers in rat-infested areas with poor sanitation. Camps were just bamboo structures covered with tarpaulin or thatch. For beds, they were given *charpoys*—Indian cots with string in place of springs or planks.

Two and a half years would pass before the soldiers were re-equipped and re-trained to return to Burma.

Chapter 13

Return to Katha

For six months the monsoon continued. Then the rains started to abate and the sun sent pale tendrils towards the watery earth. Droplets hung on the thatched roof like a necklace of beads, still and lifeless in the wet mist.

October ushered in the cool, pleasant pre-winter months. Dad visited Katha to check if it was safe to return. The town was sixteen kilometres downstream and half a day's travel from our camp.

He returned in the evening. 'The fighting had ceased. It's time to go back.' He glared at me. 'What are you doing here? Go and pack your clothes.'

June didn't budge, so I guessed Dad was going to say something he didn't want me to hear. I slunk to our bedroom, placed my ear against a crack in the thin mat wall and listened.

'I met a couple of young Karens who were searching for their relations and anything they could retrieve from the burned ruins of their house.'

'Don't Karens live in the south? What were they doing so far up north?' Mum asked.

Dad's voice rose. 'Their family fared even worse than we did. They had been caught up in the bombing at Rangoon, evacuated to Mandalay and were there during the firestorm in April. Like us, they escaped by launch to Katha and arrived in the town a few days after we'd gone to Kyauttongyi. By then, houses that escaped the fire had already been ransacked. Thugs were still running wild in the market place.'

I heard a gasp from Mum. 'I suppose everything of ours must have been taken too.'

'The chief Medical Officer at the Katha General Hospital and a few nurses remained behind to care for the sick and dying. They carried on working, but around four o'clock a few days later, these Karen evacuees heard the sound of planes and explosions near the waterfront and the hospital. There were no ward orderlies, so the surgeon and his nurses were forced to abandon their patients and flee from the burning building.'

'Will there be anywhere for us to stay at Katha if we return?' Mum asked.

'We'll find a place. Anything will be better than this.'

The floor creaked, and I guessed the conversation had ended, so I crept to my shan bag and pretended to be packing.

It seemed like ages since we'd escaped from the bombed town.

***

Nanny decided to leave us and return to her own village to live with her parents. Mum paid her wages and she left without saying goodbye to me. I wondered why Mum hadn't told me Nanny was leaving. Perhaps she was afraid I'd grown attached to her, but I was too excited about our return to Katha and only noticed her absence when I saw Dad carrying Herman. I realised, too, that his rifle was missing.

***

In May 1942, General Stilwell deployed Chinese troops to Katha. Eight hundred Japanese died in the skirmish that followed.

Dad must have seen vestiges of the fighting when he went to investigate conditions in Katha. He hired two canoes similar to the ones we'd used on our trip upstream. The river, made famous by Kipling's *Road to Mandalay*, flowed peacefully. The current favoured us, and we were back in much less time than our turbulent journey to the camp, nearly a year ago.

At Katha, several launches lay half-submerged in the river.

'Were they bombed, Mummy?' I asked.

She did not answer, but stared ahead.

'They've been scuttled,' Bertie said.

'What does that mean?'

'The owners sank their boats so that the Japs couldn't get them.'

The last time we'd been on the banks of the Irrawaddy, thousands of people had gathered there. Now no one was in sight. The outskirts of Katha were serene. Not so the town proper. The hospital was totally demolished. Cases of spirits had exploded in the storehouse.

Houses were blackened ruins—bombed by Japanese aircraft or burned through Churchill's scorched-earth policy. Only ashes remained of the house we'd rented. The rose bushes stood neglected and rampant. A lean dog scratched its mange, watching us. Not a sound, apart from the occasional cawing of a crow, infringed upon the silence.

We plodded along in no-man's-land, little clouds of dust rising to our ankles. I thought of our trudge from the burning city earlier in the year. The road was not quite as dusty now, after the rains. Rupert pushed the loaded pram, Bertie wheeled the stroller with Herman hunched up in it.

Dad paused in front of a sports field, and pointed. 'We'll try this.'

We headed towards the grandstand. I wondered how we could live in a stack of seats. Then I saw a little house on a raised platform—weatherproof and warm, with facilities for cooking food. Dad decided to move in.

It was heaven to live with a wooden floor rather than a bamboo hut where splinters stabbed my feet. The monsoons had cleared, leaving the land fresh, trees green and atmosphere invigorating. The sky was a vivid blue, the sun's kiss warm and inviting, the days idyllic. Blades of grass danced in waves to the tune of the breeze. The Arcadian scene stretched out to the horizon. Palms waved a welcome from the distance.

The open spaces around the field were a pleasant change from the small village. Mum unpacked our belongings and heaved a sigh.

She turned to June. 'Go and play on the oval.'

Our mother was always so kind and considerate. She must have seen the longing in our eyes to run about after being confined indoors for so long.

Dad spent most of his time in town with the boys. He tried to arrange for rail tickets, hoping we'd be able to leave for Mandalay. Although he failed, he became less aggressive and told Mum our dwelling at the grandstand was only a temporary respite.

We begged him to tell us when we could return to Rangoon and civilisation.

'At Mandalay, we'll find a decent place to live. It may not be as good as our home in Rangoon, but it'll be better than this.'

Mum gave a crisp nod. 'Mandalay is one-third of the way to Rangoon and will bring us closer to home.'

June clapped me on my shoulder. 'Let's have some fun in the meantime.' She grabbed a piece of rope we'd used to tie our luggage on the pram, and we took turns to skip on the football field.

Dad sold the pram and the stroller to buy food. He didn't want to touch our British currency unless absolutely necessary. Now that Nanny had left, the burden of feeding and cleaning Herman fell on Bertie. At times, Herman smeared himself with faeces. Bertie, uncomplaining, would carry him to the bathroom. This recurring ritual caused so much frustration that later on we had to restrict Herman's only good hand by tying it down.

Rupert had no books to occupy him and nowhere to explore. Dad no longer allowed him to venture out of sight for fear of Japanese patrols. Rupert ran his hands through his hair, ground his teeth, and gazed into the distance with clenched fists.

Despite all the hardships, I loved the bracing weather. Winter was on its way. *Would we be back at Rangoon for Christmas?*

Looking back now, it was remarkable how my childish mind had the capacity to adapt to new surroundings. *How true is the saying, 'Heaven tempers the wind to the shorn lamb!'*

***

After Rangoon fell, the Japanese occupying force landed at the still-smouldering docks and fanned northwards to meet their overland invasion forces from Thailand. After clearing the country of pockets of Chinese still hiding in the jungle, they set up garrisons in cities and remote areas. The Japanese government forbade troops from entering a house without an officer in charge and warned them not to loot houses or alienate local residents.

We were not aware of these orders until much later, and worried what would happen when the Japanese found us trespassing on council property.

Early one morning, three soldiers and their captain appeared at the grandstand. Dad went to talk with the officer, and we gravitated to a half-hidden niche, peering out like mice waiting for the cat to pounce.

After they had spoken with each other for some time, Dad ushered the captain into our humble home. Kimio Kashihara was a Christian from Osaka. Mum made tea, and sent me to present our guest with a hot cup of the fresh brew. After he'd drunk his tea, the captain asked, 'May I visit you sometimes?'

'You're most welcome to do so,' Dad said.

I lingered, fascinated by the long sword attached to his belt. When he left, Dad said, 'The Japs are on patrol and mean no harm.'

The captain returned whenever he was off duty. He treated us like friends. We'd sit around while he related his adventures. From him, we learned how to say thank you, good-bye, and the numbers one to twenty in Japanese.

June was surprised to know her name stood for the number twelve, but pronounced with two syllables: Ju-ne.

One day, Dad asked Kimio whether he was married.

He smiled. 'When your daughters are older, I'll marry one of them.'

Everyone laughed, and my fear of imprisonment and torture vanished for the time being.

***

In February 1943, as soon as the railways resumed a spasmodic service for civilians, Kimio showed Dad where to apply for a travel pass. I was sorry to part from our friend but we skipped around at the thought of returning to the whitewashed house in Rangoon.

When Kimio left, Dad extracted several notes from my stomach binder to pay for the tickets. The money belt had became skinny like me. Our possessions dwindled down to the bare necessities.

On the afternoon of our departure, we sauntered across the field. The unmown grass, now grown knee-high, brushed against my legs and the warm winter sun caressed my cheeks. The grandstand had been our home for three months, giving us hope that life under Japanese occupation wouldn't be too bad after all.

'We'll soon be back in our lovely home at Rangoon,' June said.

Mum held Baby tightly and bit so intensely blood stained her lower lip. A small voice of despair whispered in my ear. *Was Mum hiding something from us?*

It took about ten minutes to reach the station. The engine hissed and rumbled. People crowded in, pushing each other, tugging at their luggage and cramming into any available space. Some had standing room only—others sat on their belongings in the aisles.

At last, the whistle blew, each carriage took up the slack and we were on our way. The engine puffed, leaving behind a pennant of smoke, and the wheels sang out, 'Mandalay, Mandalay.'

Pagodas of all sizes rolled past our window as we chugged along. Bamboo groves bowed, waving leafy green handkerchiefs, and teak trees stood tall and proud, clapping their broad leaves. My heart pounded with joy.

Within an hour, we passed bombed-out stations. Over-turned carriages peppered with machine-gun bullets and shrapnel scars lay among the overgrown grass. The jungle was already reasserting its old supremacy. Stockpiles of paddy—unhusked rice—smouldering from the bombing—sent little spirals of smoke to the blue skies, making a smudge on the horizon.

Passengers looked out of the windows, their bodies swaying in rhythm with the rocking. Some settled down and were soon asleep with the consistent opiate of chattering wheels. The earth glowed and blushed before hiding behind the purple plain.

Without any warning the train stopped and threw us forward. The door flew open and a Japanese soldier sprang into the carriage, shouting out a string of incomprehensible words. A rifle in one hand, he waved towards the exit.

We scrambled out, clutching our bits of belongings. The dense jungle hid the rays of the sun. It was as dark as night. We stumbled after the soldier, who led us along a track where soldiers stood on either side, guns pointing at us. 'Speedo. Speedo,' they shouted, and hustled us on.

Dad walked ahead, carrying Herman. June hung to Dad's belt. Terrified, I clung to Mum, making it almost impossible for her to walk on the rough track with Baby in her arms.

Rupert and Bertie brought up the rear. 'We are all being taken into the depths of the jungle to be shot,' Rupert whispered.

'At least we'll die together.' Bertie's lips scarcely moved.

I shivered. The cold night air and the effort of keeping up made me gasp for breath. In silence, we stumbled along. No monkeys chattered. No cicadas called.

The trail followed the contours up and around a deep gorge. A train awaited us on the opposite side. The guard gestured towards a carriage with his rifle, and we clambered aboard.

Even before we found seats, the engine took off for Mandalay. Dad headed for a corner and placed Herman beside him. Mum took the seat in front of him. A muttering arose among the passengers and Dad leaned forward to listen. When they fell silent, he whispered in Mum's ear. 'Katha was bombed the night we left. British guerrillas destroyed the bridge we skirted a few hours ago.'

I bit my lip. *How did the British train gorillas to use dynamite? They must be clever.*

When Mum relayed Dad's words to the boys, they grinned. 'What does a mine look like, Dad?' Rupert asked.

Bertie said, 'I'll watch for anything unusual and warn everyone to take cover.'

June and I threw fearful glances at each other. Mum clutched Baby in her arms, shut her eyes and compressed her lips.

I glanced at Dad. His face was inscrutable. A pulse stirred rhythmically in his temple as the hours flitted by. I remained silent for the remainder of the journey, but kept my eyes on Bertie, ready to shelter beneath the wooden seat if he told us he'd seen a mine.

***

Years later, we heard that on 6 March 1943, the Chindits, under Major Fergusson, blew up two spans of the three-span bridge. It was a hundred-metre-long structure and was about one hundred kilometres out of Katha.

After the raid, the bridge lay twisted like an untangled piece of rope on the riverbed. The cliff side collapsed, bringing down tonnes of rock and soil.

The Chindits penetrated over fifteen hundred kilometres into Japanese territory, blowing up lines of communication. Then they radioed for planes to bomb the Japanese garrisons stationed at Katha.

Oblivious to their presence, five kilometres south of Major Fergusson and his Chindits, we passed groundnut and sesame plantations. Piles of red chillies lay crimson in the sun. As the train rolled on, the countryside unfolded its patchwork quilt of lush green paddy fields. Night fell, and the whisperings of passengers reached me as the engine steamed ahead. The occupants of the carriage courted sleep in an assortment of contortions. No one slept, however, except Baby and Herman.

Morning dawned. It grew hotter as the train approached Mandalay. Passengers stretched weary limbs, rubbed swollen eyes and cleared throats, spitting volubly. Some swirled water in their mouths, rinsing and gargling, then expectorating through the windows. A woman combed her long, glossy hair, coiling it in a neat pile behind her head.

She lifted her arms and a strong body odour assaulted me. I yawned and staggered towards the toilet. Eyelids heavy from lack of sleep, I waited in the queue, watching the sky through an open window. My spirits rose with the sun. *We'd soon be back in civilization. What would Mandalay be like?*

When I returned, Dad reached over and tapped Mum's shoulder. 'Once we reach Mandalay, our troubles will be over.'

Mum's red eyes and the dark rings encircling them told me she'd been weeping. 'Our difficulties have only just begun.'

The hand of fear clutched at my heart. *What else is going to happen to us?*

Chapter 14

Mandalay 1943

The train pulled in at Mandalay around midday, and people spilled out. Everyone was jabbering in Burmese and I couldn't understand them. The last time I'd been at the station, I was only two. We had been leaving for Rangoon.

Hawkers squatted on the platform displaying their wares, serving their customers with one hand, waving off flies with their other. Unlike Rangoon station, no Indian porters were around. Later I discovered they had fled to India at the outset of the war. Not that we needed anyone for our baggage—it didn't amount to much.

Rupert and Bertie carried a heavy bag each as well as the blankets. Dad led the way with Herman, Mum followed with Baby. June and I kept close to them. Dad still did not have his gun. *What had become of it? Had he sold it when he sold the pram and the stroller?* I never did find out.

He led us to the waiting room. 'Remain here. I'm going to check whether my uncle can help us.' He disappeared among the crowd.

I recall the acute feeling of suspense that overcame me as we waited his return. Dad's uncle was head of the extended family. He watched over them like a patriarch, and they all relied on him for advice and assistance. *Would he give us food and a home?*

A picture of the king and queen hung above a large map of the city. Rupert strolled over to the map, and we crowded around. All I saw was a large square in the centre, surrounded by a blue path from which lines led outwards. Other lines crossed them at right angles and within them were smaller squares and rectangles.

Mum pointed to the square. 'This is Fort Dufferin. It's surrounded by a moat.' She ran her finger on the blue area surrounding the fort. 'Each side is a mile long.'

'Will we be going to the fort, Mummy?' In my mind's eye I pictured Red Indians shooting burning arrows at huge wooden gates. Somehow, I always associated forts with fights between cowboys and Indians.

Mum shook her head. 'I think Japs are living there.'

She turned to the map and pointed to a section on the western side. 'When my parents died they left me a house not far from here. The nuns used to take us for walks along the moat when I was a boarder at St Joseph's.' She trailed her finger on the path they'd taken. 'The walls of the fort are built of red bricks with a bridge across the moat on each side.'

'Wasn't Mandalay the capital of Burma during the reign of the Burmese kings?' Rupert had accumulated a lot of knowledge from his love of books.

'Yes. They had a teak palace built within the ramparts. When the water hyacinths are in bloom, the moat is covered with a purple carpet. The banks are covered with Poinciana.'

She placed her finger on a brown triangle. 'Here's Mandalay Hill, the town's highest point, about 800 feet high. You boys will love to climb it. Covered pathways go up all the way to the top.'

'Where will we be staying?' June asked.

'I don't know. Perhaps we'll be able to move into my house. It's built of red bricks, so we call it the red house. Our future is in God's hands.' Mum indicated a spot. 'This is St. Joseph's Convent and that's St. Peter's, your father's old school.' She stabbed her finger at a place further off. 'His relatives live here somewhere. They're Muslims. If they help in any way, they may expect you to become Muslims too.'

'What would happen if we *did* become Muslims, Mummy?' June asked.

'Your father may marry you to a Muslim as soon as you're of marriageable age. His relatives marry off their daughters early in life. Sometimes, even as young as *nine*.' She sighed. 'I know I've done wrong by having a mixed marriage, and I don't want you to suffer like me.'

June was already eleven. *What would I do if she left me?*

Dad returned in an hour or so. 'We cannot move into the red house. It's occupied by the *Kempetai* and I daren't show myself to them. My uncle trades in textiles. He says he's willing to help us on condition I go to mosque on Fridays, our Sabbath day.'

Shortly afterwards, two of Dad's cousins came to take us to a flat. They introduced themselves to Rupert and Bertie, ignoring the rest of us.

I soon realised that only close female relatives conversed with males. Segregation of the sexes was rather strict among Muslims.

One of the young men hailed a pony-cart and told us to get in. He climbed in after us, and gave an address to the driver. As the pony clomped along on the well-laid-out streets, I peered around. The buildings were single or double-storeyed—all built of brick. Some had flat terraced roofs. 'Look, Mummy,' I said. 'People are sitting on the roof. How lovely to play up there!'

'Many houses here have that sort of roof because Mandalay is in the dry belt and gets little rain.' Mum appeared happy and excited to be back in her native town.

Before long, we stopped at the base of a three-storey building. Dad's cousin handed him a key, said a few words and glanced up at the top floor. I craned my neck upwards. A small balcony with green wrought-iron filigreed railings stuck out from the building.

We struggled up three flights of stairs. Mum puffed and panted. When we came to a landing, she stopped for breath. I didn't wait for her, but kept up with Dad, eager to know what our new home was like.

He paused at the top of the stairs and fumbled for a while in his pocket. A locked door barred our way. Unlike other doors, it lay in a horizontal position. I exclaimed at the unusual entrance.

Mum, reaching us, and said it was a trap door. Dad found the large key he'd been searching for, inserted it in a big brass lock and slid the bolt open.

A cloud of dust greeted us. We left a trail of footsteps as we stepped into a spacious room leading to a small verandah and, further on, to other rooms.

June and I raced over and gazed down at the street. Vendors with bamboo trays on their heads, called, 'Fried sparrows, fried sparrows,' "Steamed arrowroot, steamed arrowroot,' and 'Sticky rice, sticky rice', in quavers and semi-quavers. Mandalay didn't appear to suffer from a scarcity of food.

The verandah gave us an excellent view over the city. Unlike other colonial towns, no grand buildings dated back to British times, but a tall steeple rose in the distance.

'Is that a Catholic church, Mummy?' June asked.

'Yes, a Gothic-style Catholic church. A priest, Father Lafon, who was a French count, built it with his own money.'

Throughout our stay in Mandalay, the church bells remained silent, as the Japanese didn't allow anyone to ring them. Perhaps they thought they would be used to signal British planes.

We were never far from the tinkling of pagoda bells, however.

Mum turned on the tap. A few drops of rust-coloured liquid fell into the sink. She threw up her hands. 'We have no water.'

Dad opened the tap full bore. Nothing happened. 'I'll check with the landlord. Bolt the door behind me.'

Rupert dragged open the trapdoor, then placed a wooden bar across to secure it as Dad left.

Mum wrung her hands. 'Imagine carting water up all these stairs.'

Minutes later Dad returned and told Rupert and Bertie to go with him.

June and I raced to the verandah and scanned the street. No sign of the boys. Then we heard a whoosh with the rhythmical sound of a heartbeat. 'Whoosh, whoosh, whoosh, whoosh.'

'Water,' Mum said. 'Maybe they've switched on the pumps.'

After fifteen minutes, Dad knocked. He had a special knock he always used. Three short ones followed by a pause, then another: 'Knock, knock, knock—knock.'

We did not need to ask who it was. June ran to open the door. I helped her remove the bar. She stood to one side and dragged the trapdoor up with both arms. Mum had been sweeping the place, and now she put the broom aside. She wiped her hands and went forward to Dad.

'The boys are to take turns at a hand-pump and pump the water up to the tank every day,' he said.

Over the ensuing weeks, my brothers' arms ached from the physical effort of pumping the water, but they proudly displayed their muscles to June and me.

'Feel my biceps,' Rupert said.

They were hard. I felt Bertie's muscles too.

'It's a shame you boys have to do manual labour at an age when you should be at school studying.' Mum bit her lip. 'But all schools have been closed since the invasion. Hopefully, the war won't last much longer.'

Herman was a source of continual embarrassment. He wet himself and, unless we mopped the floor in time, the urine trickled down the cracks in the wooden boards to the tenants who lived on the second storey.

Whenever that happened, a man from the flat below banged against his ceiling with a long-handled broom and yelled, '*Ye la thay la?*'

'What's he saying?' I asked Bertie.

'He wants to know whether it's water or urine.'

June gasped. 'Then he knows.'

I did the spotting and the mopping and, although always vigilant, the people below were continually baptised in urine.

Every time the banging started, Mum thought it was a bomb exploding. Her nerves were in shreds.

Dad loved early-morning walks and never failed to take his daily constitution. After his walk, he used to visit his relatives, so he was out most of the day and didn't have to endure the bashing from below.

***

The toilet consisted of a commode placed over a deep hole which seemed bottomless. It led to a drain in the basement, and made me think of hell. At nights, I sat in the dark listening to the muffled sounds of millions of maggots squirming, and the squealing and scampering of rats far below. Through the window, moonbeams threw lengthy shadows across the floor. The sinister cavern appeared in my nightmares and I feared to venture through the lurking shadows into the toilet at nights.

One night, I dreamt an angel came and said the devils who dwelt below rejoiced over evil. The heavenly messenger commanded me to gather a twig for each sin I had done, and throw them into the pit at the end of the day.

In my dream, I followed the angel's instructions. Flames leaped into the air. The vision made me think of the enormity of my faults. I recalled that, at age four, I had committed a disgraceful deed. It played on my conscience as Mum had always taught us to be honest and truthful. I had committed a theft and lied to Mum. Two terrible sins.

I had yearned for a long lead pencil. Mum only let me have short stubs, but gave Rupert, Bertie and June new pencils.

'Why do I always get short pencils, Mummy?' I looked longingly at June's.

'They're too big for you.'

That day, during silent reading time at school, only the occasional cough or sneeze from a student broke the quiet. I opened my desk to get my handkerchief. As I did, I saw a lovely red pencil lying on the floor. *A long pencil with a well-sharpened point...*

I glanced around. Everyone was busy reading. I leaned over and picked it up.

Finders keepers. I placed the pencil in my desk, although I knew the girl who sat behind me owned it.

In the afternoon when we returned home, Mum caught me with the incriminating evidence, and asked if I'd taken it from another child.

'A friend gave it to me,' I protested.

'You should have left the pencil where you found it.' Mum's look was reproachful.

How does Mum know what really had happened? Can she read my mind? I shuddered.

The next day, I put the pencil down where I'd seen it. The theft played on my conscience—I'd not only stolen something, but also told Mum a lie.

Five years later, I confessed my deed to her.

***

We often stood on the verandah watching street hawkers. They sold wares from woven bamboo trays balanced on their heads. Mum said it made her dizzy to look from such a height, and wouldn't join us.

One day, seeing a hawker carrying little packets wrapped in banana leaves, our curiosity was aroused. 'May we buy one?' June and I called out.

Mum joined us on the balcony. 'What do you want?'

We pointed to the tray.

Obviously feeling dizzy because of the height, Mum remained as far back from the railings as possible. 'They're steamed rice cakes.'

'Can you buy one for us?' we both cried in unison.

'They sound wonderful,' June murmured, seeing Mum hesitate.

'Yes. They're quite palatable.'

'Mummy, may we call her? May we?' June pleaded.

'Perhaps after the war. Money is running low. We have just enough to buy our ration of food to keep body and soul together.'

Our voices rose. 'Oh, Mummy.'

'I'll buy a packet each when Daddy is working again.'

My face fell. 'Promise.'

'I promise.' Mum wiped her eyes and returned to her sewing.

'A stitch in time saves nine.' Mum seemed to be always mending our clothes and letting down hems. We grew so fast.

***

Around Christmas in 1943, Allied aircraft made numerous raids over Mandalay. The old building rocked from side to side with each explosion. During the night raids, when the sirens sang their mournful song, we ran half-asleep down several flights of stairs to shelter in the basement. More often than not, the planes shed their bombs before we reached the ground floor. The explosions shook the building on its foundations, but the structure remained standing.

As soon as the All Clear sounded, we climbed the stairs and crawled back to bed.

Baby resented the disturbed sleeps and cried pitifully. After a few sleepless nights, Mum decided to remain upstairs. I hated leaving them. A feather of anxiety always touched my heart.

Dad soon tired of having to run down three flights of stairs at nights too. 'We're too vulnerable and exposed to the bombing on the top floor.'

One morning, he took me along to his uncle, and asked for another place.

'What's the problem with the flat?' the old man asked.

'It could collapse any day.'

'I'll see what can be done.' The patriarch stroked his grey beard.

'If I lose my boys, all is lost.' Dad drove the point home, knowing how important males are to a Muslim.

His uncle rose, placed his arm on Dad's shoulder, and gently led him towards the entrance. 'Don't worry. Have faith. Allah will provide.'

Shortly after that visit, some relatives approached Rupert and Bertie. 'Your father goes to mosque on Fridays and visits us after prayers. We give him lunch every day. Would you boys, too, like to have *biriani* for lunch and ice cream for dessert?'

Bertie licked his lips. 'Yummy.'

Rupert held out his hands, palms upwards. 'What would we have to do in return?'

The elder of the two cousins smiled. 'Simply study the Koran and be circumcised according to Muslim rites.'

'We'll think it over and let you know,' Rupert said.

The prospect was tempting. However Mum had taught us never to place material advantage over moral conviction.

When Bertie told me, I squeezed his arm. How proud I was of my two brothers. I adored heroism in every form, and thought of Rupert and Bertie as knights- in-arms fighting for a noble cause.

Mum was more circumspect. 'What the boys say may not only prevent us from getting a better place, but we could also lose the flat.' She bit her lip. 'I'll never give up *my* religion, but I couldn't bear to watch you die of starvation.'

Later, when she realised Rupert and Bertie stood firm and were not turning Muslim, I guessed she was proud. She beamed at them.

Mum always held fast to her faith. 'I trust God to provide for my family. Religion is not just a façade—a veneer to keep up appearances.'

***

We weren't kicked out onto the street so perhaps the old man secretly admired Mum for her steadfast beliefs. He still hoped to bring us into his fold. A few days later, our relatives offered more incentives to convert. Dad's uncle gave us a lovely two-storey house similar to the government quarters we had occupied in Rangoon—large, with big airy rooms and an outdoor pit toilet in the backyard. A small garden with a papaya tree in one corner provided space to play in.

The former occupants had evacuated to Bonoh, a Muslim village, further south on the Rangoon–Mandalay Road. They left behind books of all kinds and in various conditions. Some still had their dust jackets. Others were mildewed by many rainy seasons, or riddled by silver fish.

Books are my passion. During our stay, I devoted every available moment to reading.

Mum wouldn't permit me to bring any to the table. 'If a bomb exploded next to you when you're reading, you wouldn't know.' She had no time to read or tell us stories like before. She was too busy with the housework and with Baby. With no children's books or comics available, I indulged in those more suitable for older readers—on adventure, travel, and romance. I delighted in *David Copperfield, Great Expectations, Little Women, Jane Eyre, Ivanhoe* and *Treasure Island*. I skipped the uninteresting or difficult parts, and devoured the rest. They fascinated me. I entered the world of fiction, and went to grand or fearsome places without leaving the room. I lived through all the adventures in *Treasure Island* and found treasure in some far away land.

I became Jo as I read *Little Women* and, like her, I yearned to be an author when I grew up.

Chapter 15

Life in Mandalay

Japanese officers swaggered around with a sword at their sides. Ordinary ranks wore a bayonet. Although they continually patrolled the town, they did not molest the locals. Dad did all the shopping with the two boys. They blended in, since their language ability was reasonable, and they dressed like natives.

Burmese had not been compulsory in English-speaking schools. June and I knew only some basic phrases, picked up from Nanny. We spoke a few words of Burmese or Hindustani to the servants, but were otherwise ignorant. Mum knew little Burmese. She'd been educated by the Sisters of St. Joseph of the Apparition, a French congregation, and had chosen to study French as a second language, rather than the local one. She spoke Hindustani, which she had picked up from her father when he talked to the Indians under him.

She had always kept her sufferings to herself. Now we were at home all the time, it proved impossible for her to hide her misery. The image of her sorrowful expression, as she revealed the truth about her marriage, imprinted itself on my mind.

'Your father kept me locked in the house.'

'Like a prisoner?' I asked.

June looked sideways at me, her lips framing the word, *no*. She turned to Mum. 'Why did you marry him?'

Mum remained silent for a while, studying a speck of dust on the floor. 'It was all politeness and gallantry when courting me. You know ... A white knight in shining armour. He took me on a merry-go-round of delights until we married.'

I couldn't restrain myself any longer. 'But Mummy, didn't your friends visit you?'

'Your father denied me all communication with everyone. He locked up when he went to work and I saw no one until he returned.'

Tears welled up in June's eyes. 'Oh, Mummy.'

'I often wondered what would become of me. Would I go mad or die of a broken heart? What if the home caught fire? I'd be trapped inside. That really played on my mind.' She gazed into the distance. 'I didn't even have servants at first. Your father's relatives prepared our dinner and brought it to us in the evening. The cleaner came in only after your father returned from work, so I remained a prisoner in my own home.'

She paused, took a drink of water and continued. 'Could talk to no one. Couldn't even send a message to anyone.' Her voice trailed off. 'When Rupert was born, we engaged a cook, a nanny, and a cleaner. As a little toddler, Bertie ...' She stopped and swallowed, choking back her sobs. 'Your father kicked him away as he came up for a cuddle. He hugged and kissed Rupert while he pushed Bertie aside.'

'Why didn't Dad love Bertie?' June asked.

'He adores the children who look like him, and especially loves Rupert. Bertie doesn't resemble him.'

June's eyes widened. 'Bertie's so clever.'

'Yes. As an infant, he recited nursery rhymes so well, but your father didn't love him. He became more and more resentful of Bertie as he grew older. My heart ached for my little son, and I tried to make it up by pouring my love into him. Perhaps that only made things worse, but I let Bertie know that I, at least, loved him.'

Mum lowered her voice, even though Dad was out. 'Your father grows worse with each year.'

My shoulders drooped and I stared down at my hands. *How could I lift the burden from my mother?*

***

June and I often gazed at St. Joseph's Convent where Mum had boarded as a school girl and, later, as a teacher. It stood opposite our house and had housed French and Anglo-Indian nuns. The Japanese had tossed the congregation out to use the building as a military hospital.

The nuns moved in with the indigenous sisters who ran an orphanage across the road. The Japanese allowed them to remain at the Burmese convent unmolested, but commandeered the older orphans to nurse their wounded. The younger ones were made to weave bamboo mats and sew clothes for the troops.

Marie Andrea, the youngest orphan sent out to work, told me her story some ten years later. 'The Japs registered my age as sixteen and employed me as the officers' tea-lady, although I was only twelve. They called me *Little Burmese Princess*, but I longed to be with the others. I pleaded for a transfer, so they sent me to work in the chapel, which they had turned into a mortuary.'

'What did you have to do there?'

'I had to keep it spotless,' Marie said. 'They brought in limbless and bloated corpses and left them on the altar until cremation. They put the ashes in a casket and forwarded it to relatives in Japan. At night, the dead came to life and dragged their bodies grotesquely towards me. I would awake screaming.' She paused, raising her hands to her face as if to shut out the visions that haunted her.

'You should've remained on as tea-lady,' I said.

Once fired up, Marie did not stop. 'I resented being ordered to bow each time I passed the caskets, so I again asked to work as a nurse. The officer-in-charge sent me with the others to attend sick and wounded Japanese. I sponged their fevered brows and emptied bed-pans. I continued working at the hospital, and also looked after the young orphans when off duty.'

Would we have been better off and not have had to starve if Dad too, had worked for the Japanese? Looking back now, I suppose I should have admired him for remaining true to his principles. He must have felt obliged to be faithful to the Oath of Allegiance he'd made to the Crown when he had commenced work in the Law Courts.

***

One hot summer day, Mr Barry, an Anglo-Burmese friend of Dad's, visited with his two girls, Joyce and Joan. They had attended the same school as June and me.

'Even in India things are not going well for Britain.' Mr Barry sipped a cup of weak tea. 'Indian nationalists are agitating for independence, urging workers to sabotage vital communications.'

He sat on one of a pair of rickety cane chairs, Dad on the other. June and I squatted on the bare timber floor at Dad's feet. Rupert and Bertie were perched on wooden boxes—packing cases they had picked up during their long cycle rides.

'If only this was a glass of stout,' Dad said wistfully, looking at his tea.

He had developed a taste for the black brew in Rangoon, when his doctor had prescribed it for his insomnia. Now, at night, he drank native liqueur—a strong, evil-tasting concoction. Every week, he sent Bertie to buy a couple of bottles from the local grog shop.

'A friend taught me how to make a tumbler from an empty beer bottle,' Dad continued. 'I placed a red hot iron nail into a bottle half-filled with oil. The nail was large, at least as thick as my little finger. I held it in the oil with a pair of tongs until the bottle broke off at the level of the oil. Then I ground the glass smooth on a stone.'

Barry admired the tumbler and twirled it around. He placed his forefinger lightly on the rim and moved his finger, feeling for sharp edges. 'Not bad. Not bad at all. I'll have a go on some empty bottles. Thought they may come in handy sometime.' He put down his glass. 'Prior to the war, the Japs made Aung San a Major-General. He and his Thirty Comrades managed to recruit more than three hundred Burmese and joined General Suzuki during the invasion of Burma.'

'The British had no hope of halting the enemy. Only the monsoons saved them,' Dad recalled. 'Politically minded Buddhist monks and the *Thakin* Party greeted the Japs as fellow-Asians and liberators from British rule. The traitors sent women out to meet them with food and refreshments.'

Barry took a long drink of tea. 'Do you think they could have taken over this country without Burmese co-operation?'

Dad sighed. 'The Japs wouldn't have driven out the British so easily if the Fifth Column hadn't led them through jungle paths during the invasion.'

They fell silent. Barry gulped down the last of his drink and eyed his empty glass. I left the room and returned with a fresh pot. A pinch of green tea leaves was sufficient for several cups.

'Thanks.' Barry turned to Dad. 'The natives welcomed the Burmese army as heroes. When the BIA became unruly, many towns appealed to the *Kempetai* for protection, but the Japs got the Shan chieftains to swear allegiance before ordering the BIA back.'

'The Burmese vented their frustrations on the Karen and Arakanese people. While the Karens were fighting for Britain, the BIA attacked their villages.' Beads of perspiration broke out on Dad's forehead. 'If only we could get some rain. It's stifling.'

He took a sip of tea, looking at the ring of damp the glass left on the table. He watched it evaporate in the dry Mandalay heat, before continuing the thread of conversation. 'The Karens had kept their rifles when the Allies disbanded the local militia, and on their return home in May '42, they cleared the BIA from their area. They were not too gentle about it either.'

Barry nodded. 'Later on, the Burmese army attacked villages on the west coast where a large number of Indians lived.'

Dad ran his fingers through his hair. 'Some fled back to India, but many retaliated when reinforcements from India crossed the Bay of Bengal to help their fellow Muslims.' He sounded triumphant.

Barry waved a fly away from his face. 'Unable to subdue the Muslims, the Burmese turned to more helpless prey.'

Dad raised his eyebrows but remained silent.

Barry's words cascaded out like a burst dam. 'In May 1942, they tore off the cassocks of two Catholic priests and beat, kicked and paraded them through the streets. When the Japs entered the town, they interrogated the prisoners.'

We all knew that interrogation by Japanese police meant torture.

Dad sipped his tea silently. We waited to hear more but Barry excused himself and went outside to the toilet. On returning, he sat on the battered cane chair that seemed to object to his weight and squeaked loudly in protest.

'As I said, the Japs interrogated the priests and later confined them in jail.'

'Things will be better when the British return.'

Barry sighed. 'I hope and pray we'll soon have peace.'

In the stifling heat, the hot breeze filtering through the tamarind trees sent us into a trance-like stupor. The two men drifted into silence with a faraway look in their eyes. I waited for them to resume their conversation. The sound of my brothers' legs swinging against the wooden boxes seemed like a drumbeat announcing a spectacular show.

Barry assumed a conspiratorial tone. 'The northerners were not the only ones engaged in guerrilla tactics. Early 1941, British officers from Singapore had been flown out to Burma to organise hill tribes for paramilitary combat.'

June and I drew closer. The boys stopped swinging their legs and leaned forward.

'Seagrim, a British officer, remained behind after the British retreat, and trained his Karen volunteers.' Barry paused and dabbed the perspiration from his face with a rag.

'I believe they used cross-bows to kill Jap patrols, and disappeared into the jungle. Seagrim's men also rid the Karen villages of the BIA,' Dad said.

'Yes, but malaria was a big problem for them. They had to survive on wild rats, with no quinine or food.'

I screwed up my face. 'Even we don't have to eat them.' The words escaped me before I had time to check myself. I feared Dad would shout at me and send me away, but engrossed in the discussion, he ignored the interruption.

The days dragged on. Months passed and rain eventually fell, bringing relief from the heat of Mandalay.

Chapter 16

Guerrilla Groups and Diverse Heroes

The bamboo telegraph ran red hot. Rumours and speculations were rife. Britain launched an offensive in Arakan about the time we had travelled from Katha to Mandalay, and the 14th Army advanced towards Burma's west coast. We heard that Japanese troops surrounded their headquarters and captured Brigadier Cavendish and some of his officers.

Feats of daring by guerrilla forces also filtered through. 'Karen and Kachins guerrillas are harassing the Japs,' Barry said, waving his arms. 'They're helping the Chindits, Major Orde Wingate's men.'

Dad smiled, his eyes settling on Rupert. 'Chindit stands for *chinthe*—the winged lion—the guardian of every pagoda.'

'The Chindits are always on the alert,' Barry went on. 'One night a Gurkha on sentry duty heard a noise in the undergrowth. Silence and stealth was essential, so he didn't shoot, but leapt on the enemy and grabbed him.' Barry stretched his hands as if about to grab me. 'He seized a tiger!'

The hairs on my neck rose. I shuddered at the thought of grabbing a fierce animal by mistake.

Mr Barry paused at our gasps of surprise. 'The sentry released his hold and waited, *kukri* in hand, for the sharp claws and teeth, but the tiger turned tail.' He chuckled.

'The jungle around Katha is so dense,' Dad said. 'Unless you keep to the paths, you have to hack your way through thick forests.'

My thoughts returned to the refugee camp up north. Once, Bertie had taken me deep into the jungle. He'd carried a *dah* and hacked the bamboo across our path. 'The natives use it for everything,' he'd said. 'Huts, hats and containers for carrying food and water.'

While we were there, a tiger growled in the distance. We couldn't see it, but returned to the camp, in haste, before night fell. I glanced at Bertie, sitting on a box, his gaze intent on Mr Barry. *Was he thinking of the same thing?*

To me, the Chindits stood alongside the heroes in Walter Scott's novels. My thoughts flitted to Robin Hood and his men. He too had used bows and arrows against their better armed enemy. I recalled his battle with Prince John's barons in *Ivanhoe*. My mind drifted away to the Red Indians in *The Last of the Mohicans*. Unable to control my excitement, I wove these stirring tales through the fabric of my mind. My fantasies were impossible to pinion. They flew upwards.

***

In February 1943, Colonel Wingate commenced his first Chindit expedition behind enemy lines. He crossed the Irrawaddy River, then moved eastwards where loyal Kachins were harassing Japanese troops with hit-and-run tactics. The Kachin hill-tribes, sometimes known as the Scots of Burma, were a warlike race. At the time of Britain's retreat from Burma, they trekked out with the army, and later joined Wingate's Chindit operations.

Because of their loyalty to the British, Japanese burned Kachin villages and raped the women. When they emasculated the chieftain's sons with a bayonet, the Kachins retaliated. They impaled captured Japanese soldiers on stakes, inserted slivers of bamboo into their penises and set them ablaze. After killing their prisoners, the tribesmen cut off their ears to keep a tally of Japanese killed.

Japanese troops hunted the Chindits, using their propaganda machine to publicise the large number captured.

Were the men who had blown up the Bonchaung Bridge when we left Katha among those caught? With tears in my eyes, I prayed for them.

***

The following year, Wingate died in an air crash. Rescuers found his solar topee, with only a few scratches on it. Fifty years later, I saw it in the National Army Museum in London. At the museum, I also learned that Brigadier Bernard Fergusson, who'd been in charge of destroying the bridge near Katha, had survived the war. He had written several books on himself and his men.

After Wingate's death in March 1944, the Chindits helped Stilwell in his advance from the north. The general whipped them like the proverbial dying horse. He did likewise with Merrill's Marauders, an infantry regiment of the United States. They consisted of a motley group of volunteers from army jails and psychiatric hospitals, as well as seasoned veterans and men trained in jungle camps.

I met a former Chindit more than half a century later. The enemy still lurked in the shadows for him. Although he had passed his eightieth year, he spoke in a whisper and constantly looked around for Japanese while relating his exploits. Like a worn-out elastic band, his nerves had stretched to the utmost during the war, and never returned to normal.

'As we marched back into Burma,' he said, 'skeletons lined the road—their bones still covered by rags. Some remained propped up against a tree and looked at us from empty orbs. Others were curled up in a foetal position.'

I can never forget his words. He made me promise not to give his name when writing about his past.

***

Mr Barry related news of the underground movement—stories of heroes as fascinating as my cherished fictional champions. I listened wide-eyed about small groups creating havoc behind enemy lines—Naga head-hunters, Z Force, D Force, the OSS and Force 101.

A special group called V Force created an intelligence network among the faithful hill tribes, concentrating on capturing spies who operated on the hills between India and Burma.

The Nagas were trained to report back if they saw anything unusual in the jungle. One day, they informed headquarters that strange men were jumping down from a plane with red circles on its wings.

The Intelligence Officer requested they capture the men. The next day the Nagas brought in a basket containing three heads. The officer gazed at the bloody trophies.

He threw out his arms. He had wanted prisoners for questioning. 'Why didn't you just bring the men in?'

'Because their heads are the only things of value.'

***

Rupert felt it his duty to harass the Japanese and do his bit. Late one evening, heedless of the curfew, he slipped out of the house and made his way to a railway yard. The night was still, the moon ghostly. The guards slouched half-asleep over their rifles.

He crept forward towards a railway wagon loaded with ammunition. In his hand he carried a stick wrapped in cloth soaked in kerosene oil. He struck a match, lit the rag, placed it beneath the covering and fled.

The tarpaulin burst into flames. Shots shattered the stillness of the night. As Rupert ran, an ear-splitting explosion rent the air.

He returned home breathless. Proud of inflicting damage on the enemy, he related his exploits to Bertie.

***

One night, Rupert set fire to a Japanese-occupied building, only two houses from ours. Mum rushed to my bed and told me to hurry downstairs. Our house was in danger.

I recall the events with complete clarity from the archives of my mind, and often replay a movie of that distant day. I shivered even in the hot summer night and followed Mum, as she carried Rose. *What had caused the fire? Had a bomb been placed in the house?*

Bertie grinned. 'Someone set the premises ablaze.'

My fear instantly fell away. *Who was this brave person?* I added one more hero to my world of swashbuckling champions and prayed he'd escape capture. I remained beside Bertie, watching the blaze. June kept close to Dad and Herman, as Mum stood beside him, carrying Rose.

Flames leapt high, illuminating the darkness of the night. Tongues of flame licked the sky, leaping and dancing like a monkey on hot bricks. Heat from the inferno warmed my lightly clad body.

The Japanese were in their loincloths. One of the men had an ugly burn on his thigh. He ordered the male on-lookers to fetch buckets of water and extinguish the fire. Smoke wafted towards me, bringing the whiff of burned timber and paint.

Rupert was already working. Bertie told me to stay with Mum—then he stepped forward to help.

Nothing can erase that night from the canvas of my mind. The air throbbed with the clamour of alarms, but the fire brigade took hours. By the time the fire engine arrived, the building had burnt to the ground.

Thinking the incident had been an accident, the Japanese did not seek reprisals. They had stored bags of rice in the cellar of their house and the fumes of the burned grain remained in our nostrils for months.

My parents were glad when our Japanese neighbours moved elsewhere. No longer did cars arrive at night, nor did we see flimsily clad young women leaving in the mornings.

I recalled the time I was woken by a terrifying scream. It rose and rose—then broke off. Two short screams followed. The cries of prisoners under interrogation and torture now no longer assailed us.

Bertie refrained from joining in espionage activities but Rupert told him about his covert adventures. He swore Bertie to secrecy until he either died or was captured.

Bertie kept his word and did not reveal anything until freed of his promise. He had a strict sense of honour and I was not surprised that Rupert confided his secrets to him.

Mum had instilled a love of truth in all of us. I never knew of Bertie ever telling a lie except once. At Rangoon, he accidentally knocked over an expensive porcelain statue of Venus. Dad asked whether he had broken it. Not wishing to displease him, Bertie had denied it.

He admitted his fault to Mum later on.

***

Nothing is more important to a child than a parent who loves them. Bertie longed for his father's love, but only once did Dad ever speak kindly to him.

When we were adults, my brother told me how he felt on one occasion. 'Dad lost his wallet and I discovered it lying on the ground among the tall grass. I picked it up and ran over to him, carrying the wallet. Dad rewarded me with a smile and a brief, "Thank you." All my life, I cherished these two words.' His colour rose and his eyes shone as he related the incident to me.

Only then did I fully appreciate how much he loved and needed love.

***

War brought jagged splinters to Dad's personality. These softened, however, once we settled at Mandalay. He experimented in the kitchen, making desserts from recipes friends and neighbours gave him. His speciality consisted of a Burmese sweetmeat made of milk and jaggery—a sweetener from the toddy fruit.

When ready, Dad called me to divide it between us. I thought of the times I had divided *barafi* on my birthdays as I cut the pieces carefully, making sure they were of an equal size. Commencing from the eldest to the youngest, he allowed us to choose a piece. These occasions were the only times I recall he acted without any favouritism.

June remained the dearest companion imaginable, and kept my mind occupied with adventures in far-away lands. She had a lively imagination and took me into a sphere of fantasy, inventing games of make-believe, opening up a world of fun and adventure. At times, I escaped with Jim Hawkins into the pages of *Treasure Island*. I read *Jane Eyre*, marvelling at her endless patience. The patience everyone now needed, waiting for the British.

Mum loved Mandalay and when Dad was out she regaled us with stories of her life as a boarder. 'The winters were so cold that the water in our washbasins froze over. We had to break the ice before washing our hands and faces in the morning,' she said. 'But summers were hot and dry. Mandalay was a city of dust and heat. Tamarind trees showered the ground with their fruit, and I used to gather them and make a drink flavoured with jaggery. People drank tea long into the night. Before the monsoons broke, some slept outdoors on bamboo mats.'

On one occasion Mum poured her heart out to us. 'Your father didn't allow me to practise my faith in public. He only permitted me to pray in the privacy of my own room.'

***

After the war when I was much older, Mum told me of the early days of her marriage. She became disillusioned on her wedding night. On that night, my father mentioned that some mothers-in-law used to take the bed sheets of the newly married couple to the waiting family after the consummation of their marriage and display the bloodstained sheet to them to prove the son had married a virgin.

My father looked at their bed-sheets and said, 'That's pig's blood. Not yours.'

A flood of remorse overcame my mother, but it was too late. Although she had legally wedded in a law court, she was not married in the eyes of the Catholic Church, which meant that all her children would be considered bastards.

As she told me this, she cried, beating her breast in a paroxysm of grief. Her tears rose like a rising tide upon sorrow's back. 'This comes of being an orphan. I'd been left well provided by my parents. I was a teacher. I needn't have married him. It would not have happened if Mum were alive.'

On hearing Mum's history, the past seized me with its shadowy hands. I had an irresistible desire to smooth away the furrows on her brow. Even though already in my teens by then, I wondered why the sheet was stained, but was too embarrassed to ask. I'd sometimes seen Mum wipe blood from her face when Dad had struck her. *Perhaps he had slapped her—she had cut her lip and bled.*

I vowed to fly from my father's clutches someday. Escape from his tyranny. I felt like an imprisoned bird beating its wings against its cage, longing for the freedom lying beyond its reach.

***

One morning early in 1943, a loud knocking at our front entrance reverberated through the house. I dashed to open it. We rarely had people call, but I still hoped for friends. As soon as I flung open the door, Mr Barry stepped in, breathless.

He usually visited in the afternoons after lunch, knowing Dad had his daily constitution in the mornings, so I stared at him, forgetting my manners. Only after I had shut the door behind him did I remember to wish him a good morning.

'Is your dad at home?' he asked.

'Yes. He's just about to go for his walk. I'll get him.'

'I must speak to him at once.'

'Please have a seat,' I said, pointing to an upturned empty deal-wood box, part of Mum's attempt at furnishing the house.

Dad entered, the lines on his forehead making deep furrows. 'What's up, Barry?'

'Things are moving fast. Dr Seagrave and his nursing staff are on their way back to Burma with the Allies. Dropped in to let you know.'

Dad nodded. 'Thanks.'

That day our worn faces wore smiles instead of frowns. Mum sang war songs like *Pack up your Troubles* and *It's a long way to Tipperrary* the whole day.

Despite that early promise, the rest of the year slipped by unnoticed. We experienced a sense of timelessness punctuated by periods of bombing and long stretches of boredom.

Mum altered an old 1942 calendar to fit the current year. At her housework, she sang sad songs and hymns such as *God of Mercy and Compassion look with pity upon me* and *Life is like a Mighty River*. At times, in an attempt to cheer us, she also burst into old war songs like *Keep the Home Fires Burning*.

Time dragged its captive chains. Sometimes, a solitary aircraft droned overhead.

Dad said, 'It's only coming to reconnoitre and take photos.'

We'd run out to watch the plane as it lazily circled above. I prayed for the pilot's safety, not knowing then, that the plane was out of reach of anti-aircraft guns. Years later, I read *God is my Co-pilot* by Col. Robert L. Scott, an AVG pilot. I realised then we'd been watching his plane, *Exterminator*, as he flew over Mandalay to boost our morale and show us we were not forgotten.

Chapter 17

Slavery, Sabotage and Germ Warfare

As the war dragged on, my boredom and frustration mounted. At times, I rested my chin in my hand and stared into space.

Dad purchased three bicycles—for himself and the boys. Old but serviceable with solid rubber tyres, there was no risk of puncture.

Rupert and Bertie accompanied him to the market, and cycled home with our monthly ration of rice and oil. At times, they went about seventeen kilometres southwest to Sagaing, and bought vegetables and fruit. They mingled with the locals, dressing and speaking like them. With their heavy tan from so much time outdoors, the Japanese couldn't single them out from the others.

So many towns now lay within their reach. At Ava, they visited the leaning tower, which had tilted during an earthquake in 1838. They went to the Kuthodaw Pagoda in the heart of Mandalay. In awe, they viewed the world's biggest book—Buddhist scriptures etched on seven hundred and twenty-nine marble slabs.

'The place is full of little white pagodas,' Bertie said as I listened with parted lips and bated breath.

'I pushed my cycle for more than half a mile across the two-century-old footbridge,' Rupert said. 'It's the longest teak bridge in the world.'

'There were hundreds of Buddhist monks in saffron robes, all waiting to break their morning fast,' Bertie added. 'They looked like a great field of sunflowers spreading out to greet the sun.'

My brothers cycled to Mandalay hill and climbed to the summit. 'From the top, people are as small as dolls,' Bertie said.

How I wished I could join them in their exploits and not have to stay at home.

***

Dad went for a walk each morning. Then he cycled to his relatives for a hearty lunch. The rest of us made do with meagre meals.

Dad was adamant that Mum, June and I remain indoors. 'If you go out, you'll be spotted by the Japs and taken away to their concentration camps or brothels. Girls as young as ten years old have been abducted to serve soldiers.'

I'd seen the *Rape of Nanking* on the newsreels at Rangoon. At the time, I thought rape meant a man forcibly kissed a woman on her mouth, as Mum had told us to reserve our lips for marriage. To me, brothels represented places where women allowed men to fondle them. I was terrified at the prospect of Japanese impounding us in a concentration camp.

To make us look younger and prevent us being dragged off by the Japanese, Dad gave June and me short, boyish haircuts and kept us indoors. One day, however, he sent me out with Bertie to visit a distant cousin of his. Mum dressed me in a pair of Herman's shorts and a shirt she'd saved when we left Rangoon.

At that time, the expectation of a good meal at our relatives mattered less to me than the joy of being outdoors. As Bertie sped through the streets with me sitting on the horizontal crossbar, the wind fanned my face and hair. The fresh air aroused a sensation of euphoria.

I've never forgotten that ride with Bertie on his bicycle. I imagined myself in Rangoon, and my mind wended its way back to those carefree days. On Saturday afternoons, Dad sometimes used to drive us to the Royal Lakes—several acres of parkland not too far from the city. There, I rode on a green-and-cream cycle while the rays of the setting sun lit the trees with a radiant smile. Sounds of mirth and music from picnickers arose like a distant murmur on the air, mingling with the songs of birds. Fun and laughter had filled our day.

***

When we arrived at our relative's house, our hostess greeted us with a smile and the traditional Muslim greeting, '*Salam Ali Kum.*'

'*Ali Kum Salam,*' we responded as Dad had instructed. I removed my footwear.

'Have you had lunch?' our hostess inquired.

Bertie shook his head.

'Please sit.' She went into the kitchen.

Except for a low table in the centre and several cushions scattered around, the carpeted floor was bare of furniture. Bertie sat on a cushion and propped himself up against the wall. I did the same. The sound of cooking pots being opened and the delicious aroma of spices drifted out to us.

The lady brought out a tray laden with a bowl of rice and dishes of curry, spread a cloth on the table, and placed clean plates before us. Fragrant clouds of steam arose from each dish. My stomach growled.

'Please eat.' She placed a silver receptacle half-filled with water on the table. Then moving back a few paces, she sank down upon a cushion.

Did the bowl contain water for drinking? I glanced at Bertie for directions.

As a guest in a Muslim house, he followed their customs and dipped his fingers into the bowl. With his eyes, he signalled me to do the same. Then he commenced eating with his fingers.

I ate silently, relishing every mouthful. Our hostess kept telling us to fill our plates, but we needed no urging. I forgot all the lessons of politeness Mum had drummed into us, and only thought of the food in front of me.

Our relative smiled, obviously glad Dad had taught us Muslim customs. We had removed our shoes when entering the house, eaten with our fingers and not left a grain of rice on the plate.

***

Dad's grandfather had migrated from Persia, settled in India and wedded an Indian girl. Later, he moved on to Burma where his son, U Pyu, married a Burmese Muslim, Fatima Bee. They had a son—my father, Esau, and a daughter, Jhan.

Esau had spent his schooldays among Anglo-Indians, who came to accept him as one of them. Some friends called him Edward. He told Mum he clung to the name as it sounded more English and had a regal touch.

Although indoctrinated with the Islamic faith, he had never attended mosque or prayed from the Koran at Rangoon. However his Mandalay relatives put pressure on him, promising many enticements to convert us to their religion.

As we cycled back, Bertie said, 'Dad has presented you as a possible bride for one of their boys.'

I gasped. *Dad had displayed me like a horse to a prospective buyer.*

'You were the bait Dad used to obtain more favours for himself as a prospective father-in-law of the host's son. He mentioned marrying you girls off to wealthy Muslims, preferably our cousins, but now that times are harsh, he's willing to trade you off to the highest bidder.'

This was terrible! According to Muslim tradition, it didn't matter that we were still children. It was customary to promise a very young girl in marriage, sometimes even at birth.

Regardless of Dad's plans, I returned home happy and satisfied, my body glowing from the fresh air and fine food.

As it turned out, nothing came of the marriage idea. When I asked Bertie about the outcome of our visit, he pleaded ignorance. I did not ask Mum, as I didn't want to worry her if she didn't already know Dad's intentions. If she *did* know, then I had no wish to betray Bertie for telling me about it.

The house remained my prison. There were no more outings. Having savoured a taste of freedom, my thoughts frequently flitted back to weekends at Rangoon. I recalled the times we used to pile into our car to visit our aunt, uncle and cousins at the university. *Had those happy days gone forever?*

***

Each day brought swiftly changing news and rumours. Japanese-controlled newspapers claimed to have shot down many aircraft and wiped out most of Britain's 17th Division.

Allied aircraft dropped pamphlets telling us of their offensive on

Burma. Whenever a friend or a relative obtained a leaflet, they passed it on.

One morning after breakfast, Dad retired to the front room to read the news. Mum and I were clearing away the dishes when a loud knocking startled us. Dad slapped the newspaper down and answered the door. I dropped the rag which served as a tea towel, and hurried to find out who had knocked.

A Burmese official was there, accompanied by a soldier from the Burma Independence Arm. The events of the day unroll before my eyes even now.

With arms akimbo, the official barked out his order. The soldier turned on his heels as if they were pivots, and marched off, leaving me with fear as my guest.

The abrupt command warned me something was amiss. Terror stole over me.

The bamboo floor squeaked as Dad paced the room.

After a few minutes, he came into the kitchen. 'The Headman has ordered that a male representative must report to his office at six sharp tomorrow morning.' He left us to continue his pacing.

Japan had set up a military government to replace the old civil one, introducing a system of *corvee* in lieu of income tax. Free only in name, Burma was an enemy-occupied country.

June leaned towards Mum. 'What'll Daddy do?'

'I don't know. If your father sends Rupert, will the Japs take him away to work for them and not send him back? Will we ever see him again? He may have to keep working as a labourer for the Japs.'

'But why? He's only fifteen, and Daddy's stronger,' June said. 'Why won't he go himself, Mummy?'

'Because he has to look after us.' Mum held the table for support. 'Who'll take care of us if he dies?'

June put her arms around Mum. 'Rupert's the eldest, but Daddy will *not* part from him.'

Mum sobbed. 'That's even worse. Bertie's not as strong as Rupert. He won't survive.'

The door opened and Dad entered the room. He glared at us.

'Who's to go, then?' Mum asked.

He spat out his answer. 'Rupert. Rupert will go.'

The cold hand of fear gripped my heart. My mouth grew dry at the thought of losing my eldest brother. At the same time, I was glad he wasn't sending Bertie. I took a deep breath.

'Who else could I delegate?' Dad asked, as if in reply to my thoughts. 'Do I even have a choice? Should I go myself? Should we run away and hide? I can't afford to pay someone to take my place. I'll tell Rupert that, as the eldest son, it's his duty to represent the household.'

He had never explained his actions before, so I was surprised and puzzled. Only in later years, turning over the experience repeatedly, do I fully appreciate the anguish my parents suffered at the time.

***

The next morning, Rupert reported for duty as ordered. He and the rest of the team carried arms and ammunition from lorries and loaded them on railway wagons. The wagons stood at a siding over a kilometre from the station, tucked away beneath a canopy of trees and hidden from planes.

The conscripts worked ceaselessly in the hot sun. Perspiration poured from their bodies as they unloaded the cargo from the trucks and crossed a *chaung* or stream. When they paused to drink, soldiers hit them with rifle butts, and moved them on.

Rupert staggered under his load, carrying as much as he could, hoping to please the Japanese guards. He stumbled through the *chaung* with cartridge boxes, discreetly slipping some into the stream. He did the same each time he returned for a new load. Rupert worked hard until darkness pressed in.

After a meal of stewed vegetables and rice, the men were ordered to sleep beneath the trees. The guards informed them they'd be sent home once they had unloaded the wagons.

Rupert guessed the Japanese had no intention of letting them go. He pretended to fall asleep, watched the sentries through half-shut eyes, and waited for an opportune moment. Not far off, a friend lay, breathing deeply. Earlier in the day, Rupert had approached him about the situation. His friend was sure the Japs would let them return once the job was over.

Hearing this, my brother decided not to divulge his escape plans, as it would endanger his chances.

Only two soldiers stood guard, smoking. After some time, a sentry stubbed out his cigarette and wandered off, humming the strains of a popular Japanese song. Only one remained.

Rupert crawled away from his sleeping companions.

A twig snapped.

He lay motionless, scarcely daring to breathe. It reminded him of *Thief and Police*, the game he'd often played with our cousins at Rangoon. How long ago it seemed. His hands were now rough with hard work, his body had toughened. He felt quite a man. He knew he must get away before the other guard returned.

He raised his head. The soldier had finished his cigarette and was humming the tune in unison with his friend, who had still not come back.

Rupert lowered his head and continued to crawl. A sharp thorn jabbed his hand. He suppressed a cry of pain, and lay still, gathering his strength before crawling off like a soldier he'd seen in a movie.

Once out of sight, he leapt to his feet and raced home in a round-about direction in case he was followed.

Rupert returned to us in the early hours of the morning, tired but excited. He slumped into a seat, his hands clasped together to restrain their trembling. Then he threw back his head and laughed, proud of his success at sabotaging the enemy.

He related his exploit to us, describing everything in minute detail. 'I tricked the Japs and slipped boxes of cartridges into the water each time I crossed the stream,' he said, repeatedly.

We were amazed at his audacity. I relished every word, visualising the scene. *Here was a living hero indeed.*

My parents rejoiced to have Rupert back, but feared the Japanese would come in search of him.

My brother was fortunate to escape. The rest of his group never returned. They were dragged off to forced-labour camps, where they toiled on the Thai–Burma railway along with prisoners-of-war. The railway took seventeen months to complete. By October 1943, more than sixteen thousand Allied prisoners-of-war who had worked on it were dead. About one hundred and fifty thousand forced local labourers also lost their lives on the Death Railway. Rupert's friend was one of them.

When the boy was first taken away, his family mourned, hoping and praying for his return. Their prayers proved to be in vain.

After the war, his younger brother travelled to Thailand hoping to gain some news of his missing brother. There, a native described to him the fate of one of the prisoners—a young Anglo-Indian boy who died and was buried in the camp. Perhaps it was his brother.

***

Japanese ill-treatment of prisoners is well documented. Even during the war, we came to know of their atrocities through the bamboo telegraph. Japanese soldiers had a penchant for slapping. Everyone had heard of their water torture and method of burning prisoners with lighted cigarettes.

One day the *Kempetai* permitted a priest to visit their Headquarters at Mandalay. Mr Barry subsequently met the priest, who told him what he had witnessed at *Kemptai* headquarters. A forty-year-old English prisoner, his body scarred by cigarette burns, lay dying in a pool of blood. Twenty men were confined to a small room covered with human waste.

On the walls, inmates had written prayers and farewell messages in blood. The concrete walls seemed to sweat with outbursts of hope, despair and anger. An angry prisoner used his own faeces to record curses on his jailers.

After the war, I met Betty, the daughter of an Anglo-Indian official who had worked for the British government in Burma. 'The Japs pulled out my father's finger and toe nails and burned his torn fingers with lighted candles. After days of torture, they ordered him and two other men to dig a grave. Then they buried them in it.'

'How did you get to know this?' I asked.

She choked back her tears. 'Burmese friends spied on the Japs and gave us the gruesome details.'

***

All too often during the Allied retreat from Burma, the enemy used prisoners-of-war for bayonet practice. Once, a prisoner managed to escape and staggered back to Allied lines. Looking like a lobster, he gasped out his story through blistered lips.

Whenever Japanese captured a Chindit, they tied his hands, ordered him to place his head on the side of a well, and decapitated him with a sword.

Years later, an ex-serviceman told me of his experience. 'It was my painful duty to remove the heads from the wells and give them a decent burial when we entered Burma.'

Others never revealed their sufferings even to their closest ones. An ex-POW only mentioned his torture because his wife asked why the skin on his back had curious ridges. 'The Japanese tied me to a tree and tightened the wire each morning to heighten the agony.'

***

In 2004, HarperCollins published Daniel Barenblatt's book, *A Plague upon Humanity*. The author says that, in 1944, US officials discovered the Japanese government had used the Rangoon customs house for bizarre medical experiments. Branblatt wrote that Japanese units trained in germ warfare had been spreading cholera in Mandalay and Rangoon, under the guise of purifying the water.

Around 1943, we had a cholera outbreak in Mandalay. I recall my parents saying there had been no epidemics when the British were in Burma. A state of panic ensued and, whenever a bout of diarrhoea occurred, which was frequently, we suspected cholera.

Friends advised us to boil all our drinking water. It tasted horrible, but our fear receded.

Only now do I know the truth about this cholera outbreak, and I thank God for protecting us during those difficult days.

Chapter 18

Plague and Smallpox

Summer scorched its way to winter. The weeks dragged on. We waited for the war to end. To pass the time, Mum told us stories of her past while Dad and the boys went out. June and I loved to listen to her tales. They reminded us of the times she used to relate stories she'd read to all of us at Rangoon.

When the occupying government announced the opening of a Japanese school in Mandalay, I thought of our friend, Kimio Kasihara, whom we'd met at Katha. I smiled with satisfaction as we already knew the numbers one to twenty in Japanese. I waited to be enrolled at the new school.

Our neighbours, Mr and Mrs Hamilton, were the first to enrol their children. Neville Hamilton was a lawyer and had offered Dad a position in the Mandalay Law Courts similar to the one he held before. Dad refused the offer, saying he would not work for the enemies of Britain.

June and I longed to join them and have friends. We stood at the window and watched other children as they returned from school in the afternoon. But Dad said it was a defeatist attitude, reiterating he would not co-operate with the enemy, or send us to a Japanese institution.

Mum looked on the gloomy side. 'I can teach the children Mathematics and English. But why make them study? God alone knows whether we'll survive till the end of hostilities. Let them be free to enjoy themselves.'

So June and I did nothing more than eat, sleep, play and read until we had consumed all the books on the shelves.

Dad suggested that, whenever I came across a word I couldn't understand,

I should ask someone what it meant, but I continued to read for sheer pleasure. He was the first to finish reading everything on the shelves he thought worthwhile. He then borrowed books from acquaintances and relatives. Some of his friends had not evacuated during the retreat. They still had all their possessions except their cars and radios, which the Japanese had confiscated.

We re-read books until our eyes ached. I drew up my legs and leant against the wall, reading *Little Women*, blinded by tears over the unhappy parts.

Eventually, Mum insisted that I stop reading it as I cried too much.

June sympathised with me. She realised I enjoyed reading and knew how much I missed my dolls. She found two large pieces of cardboard, drew dolls on them, cut them out and coloured the cardboard cutouts with bits of crayon. She made dozens of dolls to comfort me. 'You now have more than you had before the war.'

Making believe they came to life, June gave each a distinctive voice and style of walk. I loved escaping into a world of magic wherever June decided to take me on our 'flying carpet'.

All this came to a sudden end one winter's day.

Mandalay is hot and dry most of the year. For a few months the weather is cold and dry—a time when plague spreads. The Japanese did not employ sanitary inspectors to oversee the drains, and they became magnets for rats.

An epidemic swept the city.

The local government supplied rattraps to the people, offering a reward for every dead rat brought in. Some Catholic nuns at a Shan village trapped rats and received two *annas* per head. They used the money for feeding orphans, and kept starvation from their door.

Buddhists did not co-operate as they believed in re-incarnation—that a rat might have been their father, mother, brother, sister or some other relative in a previous existence. In the early hours of the morning, they got to the traps before the rat-catchers arrived and released the vermin, hoping to gain merit and be reborn a superior being.

The occupying force registered the names of everyone within the city and gave ration cards to each individual for rice, cooking oil, sugar and salt. In this way, they kept a check on us and controlled every move we made. In

March 1944, they used this information to find us.

A nurse accompanied by two Japanese soldiers entered our house to inoculate everyone. One of the soldiers called out Dad's name, the other wiped his arm with a swab of cotton, and the nurse jabbed a needle attached to a long syringe into him.

The events of that fateful day have seared themselves into my memory.

'Now I want you to show me how brave you are,' June said.

I swallowed hard. 'I'm not afraid.'

After our inoculation, we continued playing with our little cutout cardboard dolls, pretending they had to line up for their needles. When it was time for Mum to have her bath, she called June to take care of Rose.

June left me, but within a few minutes she came back carrying the toddler in her arms. 'Tell Mummy I feel sick. I'm going to lie down for a while. Look after Baby.' She handed Rose to me, and staggered off to bed.

Those were the last coherent words she spoke to me.

Her short rest was to be an eternal one.

When Mum finished her bath, I told her what had happened and she went to June straight away. June said she felt cold and had a massive headache.

She was asleep when I joined her in bed that evening.

The next morning, she sat bolt upright, pulling the blanket off me with her abrupt movement. She muttered strange, garbled words. I rose, suddenly afraid. Beads of perspiration stood upon her brow. Staring straight ahead with a glassy gaze, she muttered something through parched lips and seemed unaware of my presence.

I slid out of bed and rushed to Mum. 'June's looking strange and I can't understand what she's saying.'

My parents raced to her. They questioned her but she lay on her back and said nothing, her eyes darting all over. Mum put her arms around June and, with Dad's help, led her to the toilet.

She couldn't bend her legs and was goose-stepping stiffly between them. It reminded me of newsreels I'd seen of Hitler's Nazi troops.

After they'd returned June to her bed and made her comfortable, Dad left the house to ask his uncle for help. As soon as he departed, Mum fell to her knees beside June and stormed heaven with her prayers. She pressed a crucifix to my sister's lips and kept repeating, 'Merciful Mother, have mercy on her.'

Within half an hour, Dad returned with his uncle and a man who carried a wooden box. Divided into sections, each compartment of the box contained powders and pills. He checked June's pulse, rummaged amongst his herbs in silence, made up a concoction and pressed the brew to her lips.

June had her jaws clenched. The medicine spilled from the sides of her mouth.

He soon gave up attempting to administer his herbs and slipped a small box of snuff into Dad's hands, speaking in hushed tones. Dad's uncle paid the herbalist, and both left as silently as they had come.

Mum's face turned pale. Her lips moved in prayer. Dad was strangely quiet, watching June. She appeared relaxed but we gathered around, sensing tragedy unrolling.

Moments later, she gave a few gasps, her head rolled to one side and lay still.

I froze at the sight of my sister, so young and active, stretched out on the bed. My introduction to death. A scene never to be forgotten.

Dad placed a small hand mirror against June's face and studied it. His Adam's apple slid up and down. Then, with a look of anguish, he left the room.

His gloom rolled towards us like a fog, plunging us into deep despair. As soon as he departed, Mum shut the door and hastened back. She crossed my sister's hands on her breast.

After attempting to shut her eyes without success, Mum turned to us and asked for two coins. I ran to my little bag and took out the pocket money I'd saved ever since we'd left Rangoon.

Mum placed a coin on June's eyelids until they remained closed of their own accord. She kissed her forehead and told us to do the same. Then she fell upon her knees beside her.

Dad's relatives returned, bringing their women with them. They filled the room and whispered among themselves, pointing to the way Mum had placed June's hands. It was not the Muslim way, but none of them could do anything about it. June's body was cold and rigor mortis had already set in.

Two elderly female relatives took charge of preparing my sister for burial. They sent everyone, except Mum, out of the room.

When they allowed me to return, June lay wrapped in a white shroud. My mouth flew open. I threw my hand over it and wondered what they had done to her.

The men put her in a coffin, which they placed on a litter and carried off.

Dad did not allow us to attend the funeral. We stood on the balcony, watching sorrowfully. Mum cradled Rose in her arms. Several mourners, all men, formed a procession and took turns to carry the bier. Dad, Rupert and Bertie also stepped forward and supported the litter on their shoulders. The burial party moved out of sight down the street. They carried my sister to a Muslim graveyard, and buried her facing Mecca.

The roses faded from my mother's cheeks and she appeared to have aged several years. Other women might have lamented loudly. Yet as always, Mum took her suffering silently, although her eyes filled with unshed tears. Torn by sorrow, especially since June had not received the last rites or been buried in a Catholic cemetery, she contained her agony and hid her unhappiness. This was her cross. She carried it alone.

The hand of grief gripped me, causing a choking, stifling sensation and an intense pain. I threw myself upon my bed. My body shook with sobs. Too young to grasp the full meaning of death, I remained conscious of an immense void within my heart.

A solemn stillness pervaded the house. How long I stayed in bed I don't know, but the light had gone out of my life. The room had grown dark, as if a black cloud had passed over the sun. I felt a hand on my shoulder and turned around, trying to distinguish through the tears the figure standing behind me.

'Don't cry,' Bertie whispered. 'June's in heaven, you know. It's time for lunch now. The relatives have sent us something to eat. Dad's not at home. Mummy's praying and cannot be disturbed.'

His words of sympathy only caused me to break into more frenzied sobbing.

He did his best to console me, to no avail. I was totally lost. It was impossible to live without June, my constant friend. Ever since the evacuation from Katha, during the cold nights, I'd shared her blanket, her bed and her bodily warmth.

Days passed. I curled up in bed like a wounded animal and closed my eyes. Solitude became a dungeon in which thoughts of my sister chained me.

Overwhelmed by her death, I lost part of my childhood.

***

One warm, balmy day as spring approached, I ventured out into our tiny back yard. Alone in the garden, I longed to communicate with June. She had loved singing the *Woodpecker Song, Ferry Boat Serenade, Roll out the Barrel* and Judy Garland's *Somewhere over the Rainbow*.

I sang in our secluded backyard, in the hope my sister would hear me from heaven. The leaves brushed my body, the sunshine warmed my skinny limbs. I sang aloud, hoping June would return and weave herself once more into the texture of my existence. Above me, colourful birds warbled in reply.

Suddenly I felt a stinging sensation across my ears.

'Don't ever let me hear you sing again.' My father's shrill stiletto-voice startled me. My ears rang from the repercussion of the slap. I shrank back in fear, more frightened than I had ever been—even more than when we had fled from fire-ravaged Katha.

Everything started to spin. The sun, the flowers, the birds all whirled in mock merriment until I could scarcely breathe. My knees buckled beneath me. I slid down, hanging onto the wooden fence until I blacked out.

Minutes later, the darkness lifted and fragments of fear floated up to the surface of my consciousness.

From that day, I stopped singing, except softly, when I was alone. Years later, I tried to sing aloud but my voice rarely rose above a whisper. The force of that blow had driven its way deep into my soul.

During the long nights, I lay awake for hours and gnawed my nails—a lonely child grieving for a sister who had left for a better world.

***

When Mum came to be reconciled with her own grief and had scrambled over the rocks of sorrow, she attempted to console me. 'Time heals all things,' she said.

I bit my nails and clenched my jaw.

The following day, Mum handed me one of the prayer books she had saved when we left Katha. 'Without hope all is lost. Read the chapter on Hope.'

The little black book told me that not even a sparrow fell from its nest without God knowing and caring. It spoke of trust in God and held out a faint glow of hope.

Mum kindled the spark of hope into a flame. 'Your father intended to marry June off to a Muslim, if she had lived a little longer. He told me of his intentions. I'd have had to sacrifice my own daughter through fear of him. God called June to Heaven to save her from a forced marriage and probably an unhappy one. We would have lost her, either way.'

'Why did she get plague when she'd been inoculated like the rest of us?'

'Sometimes a person gets plague from the inoculation.'

That was no consolation to me. Still as I continued to seek solace from Mum, she began to unlock the fountains of her heart.

As the weeks wore on, I no sooner laid my head on the pillow than the mantle of sleep wrapped me in its warm embrace. I realised for the first time that not everyone existed in a constant state of alarm like we did, and I longed to be like other children who lived without fear of their father.

***

Not long after June's death, Dad's relatives increased their pressure to convert us. One day he brought home a booklet, *Proof of Prophet Mohammed*. 'I want each of you to read this.'

Too afraid to refuse, Rupert, Bertie and I took turns reading it. I slouched against a wall and went through it as rapidly as I could. Then I returned it to Dad.

His eyes searched my face as he took it back. 'Have you read it?'

'Yes.' I moved away as fast as I could.

'Can you recite the *shahada*, the statement of belief in Allah?'

I nodded. During the first bombing at Rangoon, I'd heard my grandmother repeat the *shahada* while in the trench, and knew it word for word.

'Say it,' he commanded, his voice rising in excitement.

I rattled out the words for him.

'Repeat it every night before falling asleep.'

Then he turned to Mum. 'Read this for me. Go through it with an open mind. You don't have to believe. Just read it.'

She hesitated and compressed her lips but held out her hand. I guessed Mum had sealed her angry protest, knowing if she refused he would thrash her.

Later, when we were alone, she confided it would make life more tolerable for us if she became a Muslim. Yet she couldn't deny her faith and face eternal damnation.

Looking back, I realise Dad could have coerced her to convert, even if he was unable conquer her feelings and beliefs. *What made him desist? Did he possess a sense of honour? Did he love her in his own way?*

Scarcely had we completed reading *Proof of Prophet Mohammed*, when Rose, now three, burned with fever. Her body broke out in spots. Dad called the herbalist again. Every one waited, impatient to hear his verdict. His prognosis was smallpox—the deadly disease that left victims' skins pitted with scars if they survived. I stiffened. *Not another death so soon after June!*

The herbalist told Mum to lick the rash on Rose's face, especially around her eyes, to prevent sores and loss of sight. Then he ordered them to remain isolated from the rest of us in a separate room, as smallpox is highly contagious.

Mum followed all instructions.

The period of waiting wore on, long and monotonous. Separated from my mother and little sister, the hint of death drove me to despair. My precious cut-outs remained untouched in the shoebox where I'd stored them. The books stayed on the shelves. I crept to bed like a wounded animal in its cave. Sleep remained my only solace. Time dragged on.

I didn't see Dad except at night. Perhaps he stayed with his relatives and had his meals with them. Although we hadn't adopted their faith, the relatives brought us food daily in a tiffin carrier. I waited to eat until Bertie returned home from his wanderings.

Every evening, he related his exploits, trying to cheer me. He told me about gathering with Rupert and other Anglo-Indian boys for sing-alongs. They sang songs like *Anchors Away*, but to the words 'When there's a lady, I'm after her…' I'd always been fond of him, but from then on he remained a rock I'd cling to.

One day, he took some dried mangoes from the meat-safe—a rat-proof and cockroach-proof cupboard in which we stored fresh food. 'June made these for us before she died. She'd like us to enjoy them with our meal.'

She had carved them in a circular cut that wound around the circumference, salted and sunned them. I had watched her as she dexterously sliced the mangoes with a sharp knife. When dried they stretched out like an accordion. It was a work of art. Our tears added to the saline flavour of the fruit.

***

In an attempt to re-take the country from Japanese forces, the Allied bombing increased in intensity. Dad and the boys had dug a trench in the back yard and, every night when the Lancasters flew over, we raced from our beds to the air-raid shelter. Mum and Rose couldn't come to the trench until the danger of contagion ceased, so Mum would grab her and crawl beneath the bed whenever the sirens shrilled a warning.

I huddled in fear, and prayed for them.

Late one night, the bombers flew over in full force. They came in waves, breaking the silence like a roll of thunder. The earth trembled from the roar of anti-aircraft guns and the explosion of bombs, dislodging dirt from the sides of the trench. Amid the noise and confusion, I heard a dull thud from the direction of the house. I expected a blast to follow, and pictured a bomb falling on my mother and Rose as they crouched beneath the bed.

I half-rose to my feet.

Bertie cried, 'An unexploded bomb must have fallen on our place.'

We scrambled out of the dark trench, into the dust and smoke. Mum was running towards us through the haze with Rose in her arms. 'The house is on fire.'

Around us the drone of planes, bomb explosions and the pounding of anti-aircraft guns rent the air. The full moon lit our way to the house. We raced up the stairs, drawn to a bright light. An odour, which I learned later was cordite, assailed my nostrils.

Mum stopped me before I entered the room where flames roared. She handed my sister to me. 'I'm going to help put out the fire. God will protect you and not let you catch small-pox from Rose. Look after her.'

To prevent Rose from scratching her skin, Mum had tightly secured her hands. She was swathed in a soft, white sheet like a shroud, with only her face visible. She nestled in my arms, looking angelic with her eyes shut. Fresh scars, from which scabs had already fallen, pitted her countenance.

I held her close and entered the room. The heat from the blaze warmed my skinny limbs. Smoke stung my eyes. I coughed as the fire sizzled, letting off blue sparks and orange flames. The boys drenched their beds with water while Mum and Dad doused the incendiary bomb with sand.

I was so happy Mum had escaped injury and my little sister was now on the road to recovery.

***

Next morning, Dad said, 'I'm going for my daily walk. The relatives will bring in your evening meal.'

As soon as he left, Mum beckoned to us. 'Sit down and let me tell you what actually happened last night.' Her eyes glistened. 'When the bombers razed the city, Rose, in her delirium, trilled out the hymn, *Father, we thank Thee for the Night*. My heart beating wildly, I dropped to my knees. "Thank you, God, for saving my child," I said.'

She shook her head sideways. 'If my faith had wavered when I witnessed the family sick and starving, this sign from Heaven only served to strengthen me. I rose, my trust in the Lord restored. As the bombs exploded, I held Rose to my breast and hid in the makeshift bomb-shelter beneath the dining table. Crouching low, I used my body as a shield. I prayed aloud as the planes roared above. The house shuddered with the vibration from their engines. I waited for an explosion but only heard a thud followed by a sizzling, like a fire, from the next room.

Mum clasped her hands and looked heavenward. 'Still holding on to Rose, I rushed towards the sound. As you already know, an incendiary bomb had exploded and burst into flames just between the boys' beds.'

I gripped the arms of my chair and gasped. *Surely the Lord had performed two miracles for us that night. Not only had he cured my sister from a deadly disease, but he had saved my brothers from death by ensuring they were safe in the trench before the bomb had landed.*

I thanked God, grateful we had not succumbed to the temptations of turning Muslim for the sake of a few delicious meals and ice cream for dessert!

***

The grey army blankets Dad had bought from the black market at Katha had holes where the fire had scorched them. Mum cut off the charred parts and taught me how to patch the blankets with the pieces that remained intact. 'My eyes are not as strong as yours, and I can no longer see very well.'

She was only thirty-nine, but her sight had dimmed from lack of proper nutrition.

Glad to be of some use, I tried my best to patch them. They served to keep Rupert and Bertie warm until the war ended.

As the months passed, Rose's health improved. She was now the loved and pampered child. One day I found a teddy bear pattern from an old magazine and, as I could now sew, I made her a teddy bear for Christmas from scraps of material.

Dad's gift to her was a clay tea set. I tried to brighten my young sister's life by playing imaginary games with her as June had done for me. Rose and I poured make-believe tea into the clay cups, pretending to savour the sweet drink.

Chapter 19

The Battle of the Box

In February 1944, a month before June's death, the Allied 14th Army landed at Arakan, on the south-west coast of Burma. Japanese forces attacked the Allies and captured two officers. However the general escaped, and held on until reinforcements arrived in early March.

The main action lasted only three weeks, and we only heard of it months later. When Allied planes dropped pamphlets informing us of the first major Japanese defeat in Burma, we rejoiced at the good news. By the end of 1944, the Chindwin River was the only barrier dividing the British and Japanese forces.

***

Mr Barry no longer came to visit us.

'I wonder if he has joined the guerrilla forces,' Rupert said one day. 'Let's go over to his place and get some news of him.'

When they cycled over they only found Mrs Barry and the two girls, Joyce and Joan, at home.

'Dad's visiting friends in some distant village,' Joyce said.

Thinking he'd gone to join the Chindits, Rupert attempted to gain more information.

Joyce shrugged her shoulders. 'Let's have a sing-along.'

Rupert guessed she wanted to change the conversation, but Bertie could never resist a song. He produced his mouth organ. 'What would you like to sing?'

The girls sang a parody of *There's Gold in the Mountains*. My brothers joined in, forgetting the main purpose of their visit.

The words of the parody ran:
Knees up, Mother Brown,
Your drawers are falling down,
Knees up, knees up,
Don't let the breeze up,
Knees up, Mother Brown.

Bertie told me all about it when they returned home. When I sang it, Mum said I was never to sing a naughty song again.

***

The year shuddered by, and we ran short of money. The lump sum we'd received from the British government at the commencement of war had now diminished to one or two notes. Even *I* realised the need to conserve what little was left.

Aware of our dire need for cash, Rupert told Dad he wanted to find employment.

Dad remained silent for a while, then nodded. '*I* won't work for the Japanese, but *you* may look for a job.'

A Japanese bank employed clerks to count crate loads of currency solely for occupied territories. Although worthless in world markets, they used the money for paying their employees.

Rupert found work there, and received wages as well as extra rations. He learned how to count the notes fast and tie them into bundles of a thousand. A guard stood by watching, but Rupert sought every opportunity to sabotage the enemy. Whenever possible, he slipped a few bank notes away.

The day the loss was discovered, Japanese military police lined up the bank clerks for questioning. When my brother's turn arrived, they threatened him, saying, 'Japanese sword is sharp.'

Rupert's fear titillated rather than terrified him. 'But my neck is tough,' he murmured.

The *Kempati* did not realise my brother was being defiant, because he bowed and appeared submissive. They ignored him and continued to interrogate the others.

Rupert sensed he may eventually be discovered. Because I wore the money belt around my waist, he decided to reveal his secret to me. After work one evening, he led me to our air-raid shelter. 'I've dug out a hole in the walls of the trench and filled it in with bricks. Behind them are several thousand Japanese dollars wrapped in waterproof material. Every now and then, I've been sneaking some into Dad's wallet.'

He removed a brick to expose a wad of notes covered by green and brown waterproof material he'd cut off from the sheet Mum used on Herman's bed. 'Tell Dad about the money if I don't return from work one day. If I die, I'll come back to tell you whether there's a hell or not.'

I stared aghast, unable to speak. I knew the military police would torture and kill him if they discovered he'd been stealing their money. I couldn't bear the thought of losing another member of my family.

Rupert placed his hand on my shoulder. 'You tell me whether there's a hell if you die first.'

I brightened up. *Perhaps he'd outlive me after all.* We shook hands, making a pact that the first to die would visit the other.

I'd always thought of Rupert as the hero of our family. He was ever the brave and daring one, and now he was about to sacrifice his life for us. The foul breath of fear tainted the remainder of the day.

That night, the weight of my sorrow overwhelmed me. I tossed and turned—my thoughts wrenching me back from the brink of sleep. My heart was a big twisted knot.

I confided the secret to Mum the next day, when Rupert went to work. She wrung her hands. 'We must get him away from the dangerous situation he's in. The only way out is to inform Dad about the hidden bank notes.'

I didn't wish to break my promise to my brother, but I saw her point, and agreed to let her tell Dad.

In fear and trembling, she told him all before he left for his morning walk.

Dad went out as usual that morning, and Bertie remained away from home too.

That was the longest day in my life. *Will the police capture Rupert and torture him? Will I ever see him again?* I prayed hard. Mum said there was nothing else we could do.

When Rupert returned from work, I ran to meet him, guilty for having betrayed him. I shuddered to think he was about to receive a thrashing but I sighed with relief he hadn't been taken away by the police.

Dad did not punish Rupert. Instead, he dictated a letter to him, saying the family wished to evacuate from the city to the countryside, as the air raids were getting more frequent and his own residence had been bombed.

The Japanese Bank Manager found Rupert's excuse plausible and accepted his resignation. He even handed him a note of recommendation for being an industrious worker.

Rupert showed us the letter and laughed. He cherished it, glad to have tricked the enemy once again. *Once again*, I felt, *the Lord had protected our family from death and torture.*

Chapter 20

Hunger at the Farm

Dad arranged to move to our uncle's farm on the Mandalay–Maymyo Road.

We had visited my uncle and aunt every Sunday when they'd lived in Rangoon. They now stayed at their farm about fifteen kilometres north of Mandalay, with their eight children. We hoped the literal meaning of the name of the village Kankauk, *Pick up Luck*, was a favourable omen to us.

Dad took the notes from the air-raid shelter, and fattened my slim money belt. He used some of it to hire two bullock-carts. Then he and Rupert cycled over to the farm.

I stood in front of the shelves of books we had to leave behind, ran a finger along their spines, and stopped at *Little Women*. I opened it and gave it one swift look before replacing it. How I longed to take it with me, but Mum had forbidden us from taking anything that didn't belong to us.

***

A pair of bullocks pulled each cart. One contained all our cooking utensils, empty kerosene oil tins, our monthly ration of rice and oil, our deal wood boxes for furniture, the mats for laying our quilts on, our blankets, mosquito nets and clothes.

Mum, Herman, Rose and I went in the other cart. Bertie tossed his bicycle in the cart and clambered in. The two of us sat at the back with our feet dangling. The cart trundled along, bumping and bouncing on the pot-holed road.

The cart had massive wheels, a metre and a half high, with strong wooden spokes. The owner must never have oiled the axles, as the wheels screamed all the way.

Every so often the driver grabbed a bull's tail, raised it and prodded the animal's anus with a stick to hurry it. When Japanese army trucks came into sight, he moved over to the dusty tracks on the side. We choked from the dust the ambling bullocks kicked up.

We passed several pagodas. Some were solid brick structures; others were wooden whitewashed ones no higher than two metres. I recalled the last time we had driven on the Rangoon–Mandalay Road. How much had happened since we fled to the refugee camp. June had still been with us and I'd thought we were going for an extra holiday.

Even now, my childish optimism persisted. Happy at the prospect of moving to the farm and meeting my cousins, I anticipated fun with them and my two brothers. I imagined us playing hide-and-seek in the cattle shed among the animals or in the hay.

***

A dilapidated sign with Burmese letters announced the village of Kankauk. In the distance, the fierce sun blazed over a dozen wooden huts, huddled together like children in fear. I turned around, anxious about Mum. She gripped the sides of the dray. Her head swayed with each bump. Rose was asleep on her lap and Herman grinned at the passing sights. I detected a disgusting odour and knew he had dirtied his pants.

We branched off the track and rumbled down a trail dotted with acacia trees on either side. They had thorns as long as my fingers—longer than any I'd ever seen. Cattle munched mouthfuls of leaves. I wondered how the barbs didn't hurt them as they rolled out their tongues to pull the foliage into their jaws.

Dad and Rupert were already there when the carts creaked to a stop. They waved to us, and pointed to a split-level hut not far off.

The walls were of bamboo matting with layers of straw on the top. The small kitchen and dining room had a bare earthen floor. The bathroom was also on the lower part with a large earthenware water pot in a corner and a wooden bathmat in the centre. Two bedrooms built on a higher level kept the sleeping area free from damp.

'Where's the toilet, Mummy?' I was tired after the bumpy trail.

Dad beckoned us outside. 'See that small structure? You don't want a pit-toilet close to the house.'

I rushed to the little hut and looked in. A commode had been placed over a pit in which thousands of maggots squirmed. It stank. How I missed the clean white ceramic toilet bowl we'd had in Rangoon.

Dad's sister lived with her husband and children in the main cottage, a raised wooden structure with a metal roof and a verandah. On our arrival, we had dinner at our uncle's place. The next morning, I picked out the stones from broken rice grains, in case we broke our teeth. Mum made gruel with the rice.

That afternoon it rained and I ran outdoors with a bucket to hunt for mushrooms. My cousin, Tina, was also collecting the edible fungi. She glared at me. The farm was theirs, but she didn't tell me to stop. Perhaps she hoped her scowl was sufficient to frighten me away. It didn't.

Mum sliced the mushrooms and fried them with some rice for lunch. I swore the mushrooms tasted like chicken. I longed for Rangoon and hungered for something to read. I yearned for a playmate and to escape into my fantasy world again. June was gone; and so were the books on the shelves at Mandalay.

Dad allocated us chores. Rupert and Bertie carried water in a bucket on either end of a bamboo pole balanced over their shoulders. They poured it into the jar in the bathroom. The shaft left a red bruise on their skin.

Mum was distressed over the marks. Dad said, 'It'll make men of them.'

With the aid of a grate and some bricks, he scooped a hole in the ground, constructed a fireplace and cooked dinner—an art he learned from his sister. He boiled rice and yams or corn with some leaves I gathered from a swamp. A villager had told us the plant was edible and contained lots of iron. Not knowing its name, we called the leaves 'rabbit green'.

'There's no knowing what damage your mother could inflict on an inoffensive joint of beef,' Dad joked. Not that beef was ever on the menu!

I was now eleven years old, and the eldest girl in the family. My job was to start the fire in the mornings and put dry twigs beneath the grate. I became adept at kindling fires—fanning the flames until the blaze crackled. My cheeks grew red with the effort. The number of times I burned my fingers learning to strike a match correctly are too numerous to count.

I also kept the area around the house clean, raked the ground and removed leaves the wind sent scurrying into our dwelling. I helped wash the plates and scrubbed pots and pans until they shone. An arduous job, since cleaning the blackened vessels made my eyes water.

Mum did all the work the sweeper and *dhobi* used to do at Rangoon. She swept and tidied the hut, washed our clothes and trimmed the hurricane lamp, our only source of light after sunset. The lamp threw a dim yellow light and cast eerie shadows on the walls. It was insufficient to sew or read by, so we retired early to save fuel.

***

Each of our cousins had a calf to bottle-feed. They also had to ensure the water trough was full. My brothers didn't have a calf, even though the return on its growth would have more than covered the initial outlay many times over.

When Rupert and Bertie had completed fetching water, they went exploring on their bicycles. One day, they discovered a stand of palms and went to check whether it had any fruit worth picking.

A group of village women were scraping up sand and filling their buckets.

'I wonder why they're collecting soil,' Rupert said.

Bertie, never hesitant to make friends or ask a question, moved closer to the women as they knelt on the ground. He squatted beside them and took up a handful of sand. It was gritty, but felt slippery, probably from an oil secreted by the palm trees. 'What do you use this for?'

The younger women giggled, but an old toothless crone answered. 'For scrubbing our cooking pots. We call it sand-soap. Try some. It's very good.'

'Thank you.' Bertie signalled Rupert with a jerk of his head.

The boys collected some for our pots.

I'd been using ash to shine our utensils, but the sand-soap proved ideal for scrubbing them clean first.

'Just let us know when you need more,' Bertie told me.

***

The farm consisted of several acres of flat, arable land. A barn filled with hay stood in the centre, and flocks of sparrows and pigeons fed on any grain missed in the threshing. Tiny minnows darted merrily in a small stream that laughed its way through the property. Further upstream was a leper asylum.

'Keep away from the creek; lepers pollute the water. They swim in it,' Dad said.

A deep concrete-lined well fascinated us. We had never seen one before except in storybooks. Unlike the muddy water of the rivers at Rangoon and Mandalay, the water was cool and clear. A circular brick wall surrounded the aboveground area, and a stout wooden rafter held up the tin roof, keeping it free of falling leaves and debris. A length of rope attached to a bucket hung on a pulley suspended from a beam.

The well provided an unlimited source of fresh water. In the mornings, we gazed at the village girls drawing water. They filled their clay pots and, balancing them upon their heads, wended their way back. In the evenings, before sunset, they returned to bathe by the well. They removed their jackets and, wearing sarongs wrapped under their arms, they poured buckets of water over each other or on themselves. The wet cloth clung to their bodies, revealing their well-rounded contours.

Dexterously holding their sarongs with one hand, the girls made a miniature tent for privacy and lathered themselves with soap. Finally, they slipped a fresh sarong above their heads, wiggled their hips and made the wet clothes drop in a heap at their ankles. Ablutions completed, they filled their clay containers once again and returned to the village along the gravel path, swinging their hips and balancing their pots.

***

When Dad went out for his daily morning walk and I had completed my chores, Mum allowed me to join Rupert and Bertie.

Although I lived on a farm, I was ignorant of the facts of life. Mum permitted the boys to watch a cow give birth, but she never allowed me to join them on these occasions. Somewhere at the back of my mind, a furtive seed of curiosity stole in, embedding itself into my thoughts.

One day, seeing a bull mount a cow out in the field, I ran to her. 'Mummy, a big ox is bullying a cow.'

'What a bully.' She chose not to enlighten me, and I remained unaware of the facts of life. She relied on an arsenal of sayings to give force to her words. 'Where ignorance is bliss, it's folly to be wise.'

***

As the months passed, the thatched roof of our hut grew straggly and the framework beneath the straw protruded in places like broken bones through skin. When the rains commenced, the roof began to shed a few drops of tears. Mum collected the water in empty tins, but the constant *plonk, plonk* during the night kept everyone awake.

Dad bought new straw and re-thatched the roof with Rupert and Bertie's help. Until then, the old straw had kept out most of the water. That night, the rain poured down and we were wetter than ever. The hut flooded and everyone was wet and miserable.

The next day the sun shone and Dad climbed on the roof to find the cause of the deluge. He discovered that he had laid the rows of straw incorrectly, having commenced laying them from the ridge and working his way down to the eaves. He should have placed the straw in the reverse order. However, this knowledge, so fundamental to the villagers, wasn't apparent until we were drenched.

Dad realised, too late, the logic of starting from the outer perimeter. He must have felt humiliated over his mistake as he and the boys toiled silently in the hot sun. For once, he didn't take out his frustrations on anyone.

None of us dared complain, but the farmhands who lived in the nearby village pointed at the roof as they passed, making obscene comments and roaring with laughter.

***

We were constantly hungry. Rice, even when eaten until satiated, loses its effect after a few hours and gnawing pains set in. The village had a good supply of rice, but meat was scarce and became a rare treat.

Rupert and Bertie had long outgrown their shorts. They now wore native clothes—*loongyis*.

'We'll have to tighten our belts,' Bertie said. 'I believe it helps to keep off hunger pangs.'

'We don't wear belts with our silly *loongyis*,' Rupert said with a scowl.

I tried to tighten the money belt around my waist to ease my hunger, but it only chafed my skin more.

Rupert no longer earned wages as an employee of the Japanese Government, and had forfeited the privilege of extra rations. We had to stretch our cash to the utmost. Rags and scraps of material were precious. We kept everything in case we needed them some day. They piled up.

Dad's uncle gave us a bundle of clothes probably abandoned by refugees attempting the trek to India. They were beautifully tailored dresses suitable for a teenage girl. I imagined how lovely June would have looked in them. I'd outgrown most of my own clothes, but the frocks were too large for me.

Mum picked out a white dress with blue spots and taught me how to alter it. The flared skirt and puffed sleeves hid my skinny body.

The days trailed past. We ate wild bananas with round, black slippery seeds. Mum tried to set us a good example, but she gagged every time she attempted to swallow the fruit.

She roasted garlic, added chillies and pounded it in our stone mortar-and-pestle to flavour our otherwise insipid meals. She loved onion leeks and took a bite of a young tender leek with every mouthful of rice whenever Dad brought some home from the market.

One day he bought a bundle of fresh ginger. Mum pounded a few of the roots to a pulp, then drank the raw juice. Her face flushed as she swallowed the drink.

'Why are you drinking this hot stuff, Mummy?' I asked.

'It's good for me,' she answered. 'I'm not well.'

The next day when she made another cup of ginger juice, I asked her for a sip. It burned my mouth and left me thinking that she must indeed have been very ill to take the fiery stuff.

Years later, I guessed that she had missed a period and knew that the ginger would cause the foetus to abort. It would have been a tragedy if she bore a child in her half-starved condition.

***

At the time, we had a stray chocolate-coloured pup with white socks and brown, mournful eyes. We named him Rover. Bertie had saved him from a pack of dogs that were mauling him. He had decided to remain with us, even though we were unable to feed him. It was a delight to have a pet once more, and I loved stroking his soft fur. A good, faithful dog, Rover had to fend for himself but he joined us in our adventures whenever he wasn't away scavenging.

One day, Bertie made a snare to trap pigeons that flocked to eat paddy from the haystack. He only succeeded in catching a sparrow. Rover pranced around, saliva dripping from his mouth.

Bertie cleaned the bird and, not daring to use the kitchen in case Dad punished him for wasting our precious oil, he improvised a stove from three stones. He built a fire and heated the oil in an empty condensed milk tin but accidentally tipped it over and scalded his foot.

'Look after the sparrow!' He limped off to have his burn dressed. Rather than trouble Mum, who'd only worry, he went to our aunt for help.

I knew Dad would belt him for using our limited ration of oil, and wondered whether he'd give Bertie a whipping when he returned from his walk. Mum had taught us to turn to God whenever we were in distress, so I prayed for my brother while sitting beside the stream. Two black crows swooped onto the lower branches of a nearby acacia, waiting their chance to steal the food. Rover stood on his hind legs and barked at them.

A few minutes later, Bertie returned, his foot in a bandage and a smile on his face. We shared the tiny roasted bird and he smacked his lips. 'The mouthful of sparrow is worth the pain.'

The sparrow was the most delicious morsel we had eaten in a long time.

The next day, Bertie took me fishing and, to our delight, he caught a fish. Although it was no bigger than his thumb he held it between two skewers of bamboo and grilled it over the fire.

Poor Rover drooled and begged for a bite, but there wasn't enough to satisfy even the two of us. We sat by the stream and ate the manna from heaven. I couldn't recall anything so tasty. When Dad had shot the deer at Kalaw, Nanny's dried venison was yummy. Still, eating toasted fish with Bertie on the banks of a stream with the wind singing through the trees and the clean whiff of hay drifting from the haystacks was unexpectedly happy.

A few days later, Bertie remembered the fish came from the same water the lepers bathed in further upstream. 'If ever you spill boiling liquid on yourself or burn your fingers while lighting the fire and don't feel any pain, let me know. It's a sure sign of leprosy.'

For months after, too afraid to tell anyone what we'd done, we checked our hands daily, in case the disease ate off the tips of our fingers.

***

The village was hot in summer and cold in winter. With insufficient blankets and only bamboo matting for walls, an icy wind circulated at nights. We curled up in bed to keep warm. Dad shared the woollen army blanket with Mum, who tried to warm Rose with her body. However, the toddler frequently woke up crying during the bitter winter.

One night, her cries woke Dad. 'Stop her, or I'll give the child to my sister.'

Mum took Rose down to the living area and walked back and forth, crooning her to sleep, terrified in case Dad carried out his threat and gave her away to Aunt Jhan.

***

The next day, when Dad went for his daily ramble in the morning, he took Rose and left her with Aunt Jhan. 'You can get on with the housework in peace while I have a walk.'

After he left, Mum shook her head. 'Rose is a precocious child for a three-year-old. Your father has left her at his sister's place because he hopes she'll imbibe his religion if exposed to it at such an impressionable age. You have an independent mind, and are capable of withstanding his manipulations, so he intends to mould Rose in Islam while she is still young. I know what your father is up to, but I daren't oppose him. If I ever defied him, the consequences would be unthinkable.'

From then on, Dad left Rose with Aunt Jhan daily.

One day, unable to bear the separation any longer, Mum voiced her misery to me. 'They've kept Baby for such a long time.'

'But he leaves her there every day now.'

She wrung her hands. 'I know. I know. It's just too much. She's *my* baby. What shall I do? I daren't tell your father I'd like to have her with me, but I want her back.' Her voice shook with pent-up emotions.

I took Mum's hands in mine. 'Don't worry, Mummy. I'll fetch her.'

Unable to endure her sorrowful looks, I marched across the dusty yard towards our aunt's house. She was always kind and sympathetic, realising we were caught in the tug-of-war between our parents. I assured myself she would understand. I reached the top of the stairs and stepped into the shade thrown by the verandah, my vision blinded by the transition from the bright sunlight. The silhouette of my aunt stood before me.

'Good morning, Aunty.' I bent forward towards my sister. 'It's time to come home, Rose.'

When my eyes adjusted to the interior, I saw Tina, my eldest cousin, glaring at me. Standing beside the dining table with arms akimbo, she spat out her words. 'You know we love the child. Why are you taking her home now? Your father always calls for her when he returns from his walk.'

I turned to my sister and whispered, 'Mummy misses you, Rose.'

'What's the hurry? It's still early yet,' Auntie said.

I hesitated, but I'd promised to bring Rose home. The thought of Mum's sorrowful face fortified me. I beamed at my aunt, knowing she'd understand. She smiled back reassuringly and dismissed me with a nod.

Rose gazed up at me as I wheeled around, led her down the steps and across the dusty forecourt. Almost running to keep up with me, she said, 'I miss Mummy too.'

As soon as we entered the hut, Mum grasped Rose. She hugged and kissed her with tears in her eyes.

When Dad returned from his walk, he carried on as if nothing in the world had been amiss. Perhaps his sister had told him that she would not be privy to hurting her sister-in-law.

We thanked God that my action had not backfired or ended with the usual blows and blistering words.

***

The routine at the farm never changed. We ate and slept. Nothing broke the sheer boredom and frustration. Everyone felt the monotony. Life went on.

When Dad was out, Mum said, 'I lie awake at night, and a hundred images pass through my mind. When I'd lost my parents I thought I'd die of grief but how small my suffering was compared to the present. Now I not only have to put up with a jealous and brutal husband, I and my children also suffer from lack of food and clothing. What will happen when our money runs out?' Plunged into a morass of melancholy, she fingered her rosary. 'I'm willing to give up my life if it could help us.'

Dad found the dreary life intolerable. On Fridays, he cycled fifteen kilometres to the city to attend mosque and have a meal afterwards with his cousins. When the bombing of Mandalay intensified, his uncle, the bearded patriarch, evacuated to a Muslim village fifteen kilometres south of Mandalay. Most of his relatives had sought shelter in the village during the latter half of the war.

Dad decided to follow. Everyone there was a cousin, uncle or aunt. Muslims often married their cousins and kept their wealth within the family circle.

Mum had no desire to move as the farm was peaceful enough now that Dad didn't leave Rose with his sister. She had a good relationship with her sister-in-law, Jhan, who empathised with her and never tried to convert her to the Islamic faith.

Although Mum didn't wish to leave, she dared not protest the move. She packed our scanty belongings in silence. She usually sang or hummed a tune as she worked, but now she moved like a robot.

The constant shifting irritated me, but my two elder brothers had already been to everything worth seeing around the farm and were longing for further adventures.

Dad bought a green sidecar and clamped it on Bertie's bicycle, telling us Bertie could then cycle home with the food he bought at bulk prices.

At first, Bertie felt restricted with the passenger vehicle and could no longer speed along the dusty track. He also found it difficult to cycle with the sidecar stacked with provisions, but he eventually managed to handle it well—delighted to do anything to please Dad. His patience and spirit of endurance was soon put to the test.

Chapter 21

Starvation, Beriberi and Malaria

We now only needed to hire *one* bullock cart for the move to the village. Mum carried Rose and sat in the front of the sidecar. Bertie tied Herman securely in the back seat.

Before leaving, Mum put her hand to her heart. 'I'm so afraid Bertie will strain himself and get a hernia. Pray for him.'

I kissed Mum, and Bertie cycled off to the Muslim village, over thirty kilometres away.

As he rode off, I prayed for him, even though I didn't know what a hernia meant. Then I bit my lower lip and helped Rupert carry the lighter objects to the bullock cart.

***

Hours later, Bertie returned, sweating profusely.

'Have you taken your salt tablets?' I asked. A friend had recommended salt tablets to replace the minerals lost in perspiration during the hot summers.

Bertie smiled and nodded. I squeezed his arm, glad he wasn't too exhausted to forget.

Rupert remained behind to finish loading our goods into the bullock-cart and Bertie cycled off with me. On either side of the road, carts carrying bags of rice or stacks of firewood had beaten their own track over the years.

I was sure I was headed for more misery. I had my aunt, uncle and cousins at the farm, and I enjoyed the open spaces. *Why did we have to leave?*

Bertie pedalled along, battling the wind and the dust. 'The village we're moving to is called *Bonoh*, meaning Bomb Crater.'

My heart, already floundering in sad thoughts, sank. *Was it an omen that the village would be bombed?* I pictured the thatched huts in flames like the houses burning in Katha and imagined us fleeing once again. I shuddered.

I guessed Bertie he was tired, although he had a lighter load on this trip. Even if we did nothing, we were weary so often.

We passed pagodas and Buddhist roadside shrines with food offerings. I gazed longingly at a bunch of bananas placed in a shrine for a *nat*, and longed to eat the fruit. *Surely the spirits wouldn't mind.* Bertie, too, eyed the long yellow bananas as we passed. He stopped cycling and took large draughts of water from the bottle we'd brought along. By the time we arrived at Bonoh, perspiration poured down his face. His shirt was soaked.

Thorny branches surrounded the hamlet. Villagers had piled the brushwood metres high for protection from tigers and leopards. A young man was waiting for us at the entrance to the village. He came forward, introduced himself as a cousin, said a few words to Bertie and left. We'd never met him before, but I suppose he knew us straight away as it wasn't every day a young boy cycled into the village with a green sidecar. Bullock carts were the only vehicles seen in villages.

The huts were close together and flies swarmed over everything and everyone. Dogs barked. Some bared their yellow fangs and snarled. A little way off, a child sat on its haunches, defecating. A stench arose.

I pined for the farm with its fresh smell of hay and cattle.

Bertie stopped before a high-set hut with a wide stairway and a sturdy handrail. He wiped the sweat from his forehead and looked up at a window. I glanced up and saw Mum. She hurried to meet us. Her strained look told me she had feared being all alone with only Herman and Rose.

Mum hugged me, and placed her hand upon Bertie's shoulder.

Dad was not in sight. He was probably with his relatives or, being Friday, he may have gone to the mosque to fulfil his religious obligations.

I knew no one in the village. My heart plunged.

Not long after, Rupert arrived. He had cycled beside the bullock cart to keep an eye on our goods and the bullocky. The boys carried our things into the hut while Mum showed them where to place our possessions. There was one bedroom for the boys and another for my parents, Rose, and me. Rupert and Bertie put our deal wood boxes, cooking pots and food in the kitchen, which also served as our dining and sitting room.

The village not only had the ominous name, *Bomb Crater*, it also had a dark side that sent a chill through my body. *Dacoits*! We lived in fear of them. Dad's relatives told tales of thugs setting ablaze the picket surrounding the village. When the fire reached the huts and sent the villagers running out grasping their valuables with cries of terror, the *dacoits* relieved them of their goods. In some instances, after despoiling the people of their treasure, they drove them back into the flames and laughed as the victims shrieked in its fiery embrace.

No, not *dacoits* please, God, I prayed.

***

Amiability and good temper do not come easily with near-starvation, and money was running out. In place of shoes, we wore wooden slippers. The villagers used them and, even in Mandalay, the street hawkers clunked along the streets with them.

We lacked proper food and had grown pale and skinny. Our clothes were threadbare. My yellow woollen cardigan, worn at the elbows, had fabric patches. Sewing cotton ran out.

Dad cut the leaves of a hemp-like plant and soaked them in water. When the soft pulp disintegrated, he brought them to me in a bucket. 'Comb and clean the long fibres, then wrap the thread around an empty spool. That should do for mending.'

I did so, and used the rough fibres to mend our scanty garments.

For toothpaste, we substituted salt or charcoal. Soap was locally made and plentiful, but with little money, we used it sparingly.

Dad bought cakes of soap from the manufacturer at bulk prices. 'Dry them in the sun. They'll last longer that way.'

I laid them out in neat rows on our verandah.

One day a village boy came up the stairs and looked at the soap drying in the sun. 'What's the price of one?'

His feet were bare and sores covered his legs. Flies swarmed on them, and I smelled his unwashed clothes but he grasped a few Japanese dollars in his hand.

I told the boy to wait a minute and ran into the bedroom where my father lay reading a book. 'Dad,' I said, unable to control the excitement in my voice. 'A child wants to buy some soap.'

He remained silent for a while. Then he doubled the cost of what he had paid.

The boy paid me and left with a cake of soap. As soon as he'd gone, I used some of our precious soap to wash my hands thoroughly.

For days after, children dropped in to purchase our soap. I was glad to know we were making a profit, as the money Rupert had taken from the bank now bought fewer items. Japanese currency held no value in the world market, and people realised it would be worthless when the British regained Burma.

***

Eventually we became desperate for food. Dad sold Mum's beautiful silver fox fur wrap and the jewellery she'd inherited from her mother. People knew we were desperately short of money and offered rock bottom prices for them. I thought of my beloved books—of *Gone with the Wind* and the carpetbaggers who overcharged customers after the war.

A sense of fatalism engulfed Mum. She was heartbroken at the loss of her valuables. 'I've cherished my heirlooms over the years, and never guessed they'd be disposed of piece by piece like this.'

The money from Mum's fur and jewellery brought just enough food to keep us alive.

When Dad sold Mum's wedding ring to his relatives, they must have realised we were starving, and had no more to sell. One day, Dad's uncle visited us. Before he left, he stepped up to my father and slipped a few dollars into his shirt pocket. My cheeks burned because we'd been reduced to such straits but tears came to my eyes when I thought of the food we could buy.

That evening, Dad gave the money to Bertie and sent him to the grog shop to purchase bottles of spirit. In spite of having so little money for essentials, Dad insisted on having a glass of the native brew each night. Bertie had to go out every week and buy a bottle of liqueur.

Mum wrung her hands. 'This frequent contact with alcohol may make Bertie an alcoholic when he grows up.'

I gnawed my nails. I visualised Bertie staggering home, stinking of booze with his shirt hanging outside his trousers like a tramp. Then he too would beat us up for no apparent reason.

Fortunately, the experience had an opposite effect on my brother. By the grace of God, he turned out to be a teetotaller.

***

Dad escaped from any form of sickness, whereas the rest of us were ravaged by illness. Little did I know the war was having lasting effects on him, and would start him on the road to alcoholism.

Mum had twinges in the soles of her feet. She tried to conceal her sufferings but, as the pain grew worse, she curled up in agony. Dad's aunt suggested putting a block of camphor in cooking oil and placing it in the sun until it melted.

I massaged Mum's feet with the mixture, but my efforts only gave her temporary relief.

One summer afternoon, when Rose fell asleep, Mum lay down to rest. 'Play with my hair, Hazel. The gentle touch of your hand will lull me to sleep.' She placed a fan made of palm leaves over her eyes to protect them from the sun's bright reflection.

Sadly, I did as she asked. *If only I could take her pain away.*

Shortly after, she said, 'Please prick the prickly heat on my back.'

Mum's back had erupted with little bubbles with the heat, so I pricked them with a sewing needle, taking care to sterilize it in a candle flame first. Mum then fell into a deep slumber, her arms twitching.

I lay beside her and slept from sheer exhaustion. Hunger made me tired. Sores developed on my elbows, forming ugly scabs.

My eyes did strange things. I noticed that when I picked out little stones and dirt from the rice before cooking, the grains appeared to meld into each other. Mum let out a sob and hugged me when I mentioned it. My ribs stuck out like a washboard and they hurt even from her gentle pressure, so I struggled to extricate myself from her bony embrace.

I didn't know then, but I was suffering from malnutrition and slow starvation.

By the final spasm of the war, Mum lost her voice and only spoke in a feeble tone. She recovered once her diet improved, but her vocal chords never regained their strength and sometimes faltered as she lifted her voice in song.

I lost count of the flight of time and dreamed of the past, losing all sense of the present. The moment my head touched the pillow, my mind dredged up memories of Rangoon. I frequently awoke to the howling of stray dogs. I shivered in dread and reached out for June, soon realising she no longer lay beside me.

The future seemed as empty as the long, lonely night.

***

As we grew skinnier, we developed beriberi, a nerve disease caused by a lack of Vitamin B. Our feet swelled to twice their normal size. One of Dad's cousins gave us valuable advice. 'You'll die if you continue eating white rice. You should buy wholemeal flour and make *chapattis*. Brown rice and whole meal flour are rich in vitamin B. They'll fix your problem.'

We'd always eaten polished rice because, in my parents' view, only common villagers ate unpolished rice. We switched to brown rice and soon relished the nutty flavour.

Dad bought unbleached flour and cooked *chapattis*. We watched him as he kneaded the dough, pressed it flat with a rolling pin and swirled the round *chapattis* in his frying pan. They were scrumptious, but best of all the swelling in our feet began to shrink.

Once a week, Dad bought an ox-tail from the butcher and made stew. I always had the smallest bones at the end of the tail and I bit off as much of the soft bone as I could until nothing remained.

As the spectre of starvation edged closer, insatiable hunger gnawed at our stomachs. Hunger-pangs kept us awake at night. We dreamed of meat, and during the day spoke of it with reverence.

Once when Dad was out for his daily walk, and Rupert in bed with malaria, we heard a knock at the door. One of our relatives, whom we had never seen before, carried in a bag of sweet potatoes. Without a word, he placed it on our little table of stacked boxes in the kitchen. We thanked him, but he barely looked at us and left.

Bertie eyed the plump, pink potatoes. 'Let's take one each from the bag and try eating them raw. Daddy won't notice. I dare not cook them in case he comes back before they're ready.'

I readily agreed but screwed up my face at the taste.

Within a short time, our stomachs swelled. I thought of our life at Rangoon and yearned for those days. That night, I dreamed of devouring chocolate éclairs from the Continental Cafe, and Cook's chicken curries and potato cutlets. The memory only served to make me hungrier.

We grew thinner. Only Rover appeared to thrive. Like most animals, his nose led him to food. He skulked around butchers' shops and would snatch a bone the Buddhists had thrown to the dogs. Chased by other mongrels, Rover would race home and chew on his bone in the shade beneath the hut.

I'd seen Cook make a delicious, aromatic soup from such a bone. I imagined sucking the marrow and savouring its flavour as it oozed into my mouth. I licked my lips.

Resourceful Bertie trained Rover to hand over his spoils. The dog waited patiently, flogging the ground with his tail while my brother cracked open the long bone and scraped out the contents. Then he returned the bone to the dog, gave some of the substance to Rose and me, and ate the rest.

***

Perhaps because he had wandered into the jungle so frequently at Katha or been bitten by mosquitoes more often than the rest of us, Rupert contracted malaria. He'd lie shivering in bed with his blanket pulled over his head even on the hottest days. Once he perspired, the fever disappeared, leaving him weak and listless. Within a short time the cycle would repeat itself, completely sapping his strength.

We had long run out of quinine. Dad called in a herbalist who prescribed neem tea and ordered Rupert to remain in bed, as it is imperative for a patient with malaria to rest.

Neem trees grew in profusion at the village. We picked the leaves and boiled them as instructed. Rupert followed the herbalist's advice and drank cups of the herbal profusion without complaining. The bitter concoction broke his fever until the cycle recommenced within a few weeks. His repeated bouts of malaria and his weakened condition prevented him carrying out any work. Bertie had to carry all the water for us, as well as feed, clean and bathe Herman.

One day as Rupert removed his drenched shirt after a bout of perspiring, he turned to Bertie. 'I'm sorry you have to do my work as well as your own.'

Bertie squeezed his shoulder. 'Don't worry. Everything will be right soon.'

But by the end of 1944, it seemed death was about to place its hand on Rupert's shoulder and claim him.

***

In Europe, Stalin's army was recapturing towns from the retreating Germans, and the Allied forces had swept across the Channel for the Normandy landings.

By June 1944, the Allies fought off the Japanese offensive begun in March against Imphal and Kohima. Wingate's Special Force of nearly twenty thousand men had already entered Burma. Stilwell and his Chinese forces too had commenced a pincer movement against the Japanese in the Hukawng Valley in the northeast.

During May, Karen guerrilla forces blew up bridges and ambushed the enemy in the south. Merrill's Marauders, a US brigade, made their way north. They suffered from cholera and dysentery so much they cut holes in their pants so they did not have to stop during their advance into enemy territory.

At the end of that year, US officials discovered ampoules containing cholera bacteria. Japanese planes had dropped them to infect Allied forces. No wonder Merrill's Marauders were so afflicted.

***

The volume of news drifting through to us increased ten-fold. We heard that the Allies used parachutes made of jute. I had visions of the chutes tearing in the sky and soldiers dying as they hit the ground. To my immense relief, I learned later the jute parachutes had only been used to drop supplies, not men.

The Japanese-controlled newspapers declared that British forces had been defeated at Kohima. The news was as devastating as a tsunami. Dad's hopes plummeted and depression haunted him. Shattered in spirit and sick to his heart's core, he drank more heavily, becoming even more aggressive. No matter how scarce money was, he spent it on drink.

One day he wrapped his hand around a large piece of wood, and struck Mum with it on her back. I heard the crack as it hit her bone, and winced at her cry of pain. My heart filled with hate and despair.

Time slowed and slurred. Mum tried to dredge up her strength. She moved around as though in a nightmare. Rupert remained in bed, convalescing between bouts of malaria. Bertie wandered off alone. My spirits drooped like a wilted flower in the hot sun.

***

Our despair turned to delight when Allied planes dropped leaflets at Mandalay announcing thirty thousand Japanese casualties in their attempt to invade India via Kohima. The pamphlets informed us the United States of America was preparing an assault on the Japanese mainland and the war would soon be over. Victory was in sight.

Mum told us to pray Rupert lasted long enough to receive proper treatment for the illness.

I prayed incessantly, and imagined Rupert well and strong again. I thought of our home at Rangoon and pictured living there once more.

We'd collect our car, which I expected was safely stored somewhere. I'd be back with my dolls, books and toys. The only difference in my world would be that June would no longer be with me, and *I'd* be the big sister.

The future was to prove how wrong I was.

Chapter 22

Return to Mandalay

When Allied planes dropped leaflets on towns and villages, we'd rush out of our homes. Like snowflakes, the pamphlets drifted down to land lightly in waiting arms. We perused them and passed them on, at the risk of being caught by the Japanese. The leaflets made me think of kite fights I'd seen in Rangoon. When a kite was cut off, a crowd would race to catch it as it floated to the ground.

'Did you know the British have constructed a Bailey bridge, and crossed the Chindwin into Burma?' a friend said. 'It's the biggest in the world.'

'Elephant Bill, a British timberman working in Burma when war broke out, used elephants to take his men across the river,' another told us.

A few weeks later, we read of the Jeep Railway, where American engineers had fitted flanged metal wheels to their jeeps and driven them on the Myitkyina line. My heart sang.

Mum sent me out for walks along the rough tracks between the fields of peas and beans. 'It's not healthy to keep you cooped up in the hut all day. You and Rose need exercise. Soon the monsoons will break, and you'll be unable to go outdoors.'

I knew the Allies were fighting just a few kilometres away and I wanted to help them in case they couldn't make themselves understood. I longed to meet a soldier, and imagined myself hiding him from the Japanese and from Dad. I'd only let Mum and my brothers know where he hid.

Hunger continued to gnaw, and whenever we passed a field of peas, I stooped to pick a handful for our dinner.

One day, an Anglo-Indian girl, Dorothy, who also lived in the village, ran down the steps of her hut and joined us as we passed. She wore a native sarong, but her fair hair and light complexion betrayed her European origins.

'I live here with my grandmother.' She pointed to the hut. 'I often hear your brother play a mouth organ.'

'He loves music and he sings too,' I replied.

'He plays the *Merry Widow Waltz*, but I've never heard him singing the aria.'

'We don't know the words.'

'I have them at home somewhere.' The next day, Dorothy gave me the words written on a piece of paper. Bertie sang the song—it was so romantic and gave me little thrills of pleasure.

Did Dorothy have a secret admiration for him?

Days passed.

She joined us every morning when we passed her grandmother's house. I began to look forward to my daily walk, but the sight of her blonde hair appeared to provoke the villagers. One day, a villager hurled abuse at us. Dorothy let forth a stinging reply. I didn't understand them but, by their tones, I knew they weren't complimenting each other.

On my return, I mentioned the incident to Mum. Fearing the Burmese would grow violent towards us, as so many had done when Britain was retreating from Burma, she advised me not to pass Dorothy's hut any longer. I regretted mentioning it. After the loss of June, I had no companions and liked chatting with Dorothy. I missed her sorely.

***

By the end of June 1944, the Japanese retreated from Northern Burma. Their line of defence extended south of the Irrawaddy River at Mandalay.

Late in February 1945, a far-off droning like thousands of bees woke us from our sleep. The sound increased to a frightful roar. The RAF had arrived.

Aircraft came and went all day from first light to dark. Dive-bombers accompanied the heavy Lancasters. They made a high-pitched screeching sound as they dived and machine-gunned, letting off a stream of bombs. The explosions grew more audible as each successive plane unloaded its deadly cargo on the suburbs of Mandalay.

When Allied aircraft commenced bombing the city, many people evacuated to hamlets outside a fifteen-kilometre radius of Mandalay. The Bishop, thinking villages would be safe from air strikes, arranged for priests to live in the leper asylum. However, fighting broke out when a small force of British soldiers occupied a rice-mill in the grounds of the leper asylum, and the Japanese commenced shelling.

Soon a battle raged within the precincts of the leper colony. It was close to our uncle's farm back at Kankauk. The booming of the guns sounded in the distance, even though we were thirty kilometres away. During a church service on 16 March 1945, a shell burst in their midst, killing one of the priests.

The news reached us the next day.

'The British are in the grounds of the leper colony, only a few miles south of auntie's farm,' Bertie said.

'Will they win?' I asked.

'Of course they'll win.' He made the victory sign. 'They now have aircraft and guns, and have already taken northern Burma.'

'Are they in Katha?'

Bertie nodded.

'I wish we hadn't left it,' I said. 'Then we'd be free from the Japs.'

When the sun sank beneath the horizon and spread a dark mantle over the village, the sound of shells and the roar of trucks broke the stillness of the night. Convoys, like one continuous caterpillar humping up and down the Burma Road, trucked Japanese re-enforcements to the northern frontline and returned with casualties to hospitals in Mandalay.

One night I heard explosions just over the hill. A rush of blood to my head caused a little light-headedness. My heart hammered in rhythm with the pounding of guns. The thudding triggered the thought that the name, *Bomb Crater*, presaged some sort of an ill omen, and a dark cloud obscured my troubled consciousness.

Day by day the thunder of twenty-pounders grew closer and louder.

Allied forces crossed the river just south of Mandalay and, cutting off all road access towards the city, they commenced a barrage of shelling.

Shells roared and trucks rolled past. Life in the village carried on with its never-ending monotony.

***

Years later, I learned America wanted to reopen the Burma Road to transport military supplies into China to help them fight the Japanese. However, Churchill was intent on bypassing Burma, and regaining Malaya and Singapore. Fortunately for us, the US president managed to persuade him to concentrate on Burma first.

Because of America's efforts to reconquer Northern Burma before the rest of South East Asia, Mandalay fell early in 1945. If the Allies had postponed retaking Mandalay for a few months, many of us would have succumbed to starvation and sickness. Rupert would surely have died from malaria. Once again, I sense the hand of God on us, saving us from further tragedy.

That year was full of hope and despair. Charles Dickens's words, 'It was the best of times, it was the worst of times, it was the age of wisdom, it was the age of foolishness ... we had everything before us, we had nothing before us,' were an apt description of Burma towards the end of World War II.

Hopes rose; rumours were rampant that the Japanese would soon leave and everyone could return to their homes—assuming they'd survived the bombing. Anglo-Indians and Anglo-Burmese hoped to continue under British rule. Most Burmese wanted self-rule; the whole country longed for freedom from poverty and repression.

I dreamed of the old days and not of the *New Burma* people spoke about.

Dad assured us the war was all but over and, knowing Japanese currency was practically worthless, he spent the last of our Japanese notes.

February slid into the hot days of March. One sweltering day, Rupert lay in bed shivering with malaria, a blanket covering his head. Mum sat beside him, weak and famished. Dad was out.

Bertie, Rose and I waited for Rover to bring us a bone. We paced listlessly beneath the hut, which was built on stilts. Bertie gazed into the distance, his head to one side, as though he was trying to listen.

An uplifting sound echoed across the plains. We had heard it every New Year's Day in those wonderful days before the war.

The skirl of bagpipes stirred the very core of my soul. Even now, I can shut my eyes and call to mind that glorious day. My pulse raced and, by the way my sister tightened her grip on my hand, I knew she was afraid. The sound was strange to her ears.

'It's the British!' Bertie streaked off, swift as an arrow, in the direction of the main road.

'Come on, Rose.' I held her hand and raced after him.

We rushed towards the call of the bagpipes, drawn like pieces of metal to a magnet. Bertie followed the haunting sound, cutting across fields, heedless of village dogs baying in competition with the music. Fields gave way to bushes, and soon we came to a row of trees lining the Mandalay–Maymyo Road.

Kilt-clad Scots, replete with bagpipes and kettledrums were followed by a large contingent of British soldiers marching abreast. Magnificent in full uniform, they left no doubt they were the victors. A thrill ran up my spine.

The whole village appeared to have turned out, standing on either side of the road. They gaped at the soldiers. Bertie found a place for us in front to watch the march. We skinny, ragged children stood in breathless silence while the stirring sound of martial music filled the valley and resounded over the plains.

I gazed through a film of tears. Did these smart soldiers trudge out of Burma, weary and footsore, four long years ago? To my childish eyes, every soldier was a hero.

After a fine display of strength, a sergeant gave the order to halt, and the men commenced to set up camp not far from the village. We overheard the officer-in-charge ask the headman to bring all Anglo-Indians and Anglo-Burmese to meet him, and we ran home to give Mum the good news.

The headman sent a messenger to relay the information to Dad. He told us to report to the officer, cautioning Mum not to ask for anything. She immediately discarded her *loongyi* and wore her prettiest dress.

Bertie escorted us to the camp. On the way, he told us the captain had showered Dorothy with chocolates, cheese and tins of bully beef. I rubbed my hands, imagining of the sweet flavour of chocolate. I felt its velvety texture in my mouth and couldn't wait.

Mum's voice interrupted my thoughts. 'Your father thinks the officer would expect some favour in return for food. The mere thought is preposterous.'

I was too happy to try to fathom her meaning, and only years later, did it hit me.

Bertie spoke to a sergeant, who pointed to an officer seated on a tree stump. A few soldiers stood guard. Further off, a group of Burmese craned their necks in an effort to catch the conversation.

Slim and handsome, the captain wore a moustache like Errol Flynn. When we approached, he stood and shook hands with Mum. *If only he would shake hands with me!* But he didn't even glance my way.

He asked whether we needed anything, but Mum said, 'I'm just so happy to see you.'

We need food, I wanted to scream. *We're starving.*

I bit my tongue. I was terrified to go against Dad's wishes. Among the villagers who crowded around us were many of his relatives, who spied on us and would report every word to him.

After the interview, I remained behind with Bertie while Mum returned to the hut with Rose. We stood beneath the shade of a tamarind tree and watched the soldiers operate their guns. The day was hot and perspiration poured down their shirtless torsos as they worked. I admired their rippling muscles.

Gunners milled around the twenty-pounders. I recalled the newsreels I'd seen so long ago, and I visualised them feeding shells into the guns' iron throats.

The guns spat out fire like great dragons. I put my fingers to my ears and chuckled when Bertie told me the men were firing at the Japanese in Mandalay.

That evening, we returned to the hut without a care in the world. Dad had somehow managed to obtain mepacrine tablets for Rupert's malaria, and he was sleeping soundly.

By lunchtime the following day, he rose from bed, looking like a ghost.

His skin was yellow and he appeared to have grown taller. Mum placed two buckets of water in the sun for him and, after a hot bath, he joined us for lunch. He ate his share of ox-tail stew and *chapatti* and licked his lips without taking his eyes off the food. He didn't speak a word, but his appetite had returned, and his indomitable spirit renewed.

***

Mandalay continued to remain in enemy hands. In later years, I learned the Japanese emperor had ordered his soldiers to defend it to the death.

Street-by-street, suburb-by-suburb, the Allies slowly pushed forward. On 8 March 1945, they cleared the enemy from the Catholic areas of St. Michael's and St. Peter's. During the battle, aircraft swooped down and bombed the Burmese convent. It burst into flames. The nuns and girls, who were sheltering in the trenches, rushed out, raced for buckets of water and put out the blaze. Then they fled to the Catholic quarter, knowing it was already in British hands.

They ran into a fierce battle near the Cathedral and St Joseph's Convent. The Japanese had utilised this as a military hospital. Enemy snipers shot at Allied troops, and in return, the Allies used flame-throwers and grenades to flush them out.

The tarmac sizzled. Houses were ablaze and the road littered with debris, burning timber and corpses. Like spectral arms, flames reached out to the fleeing orphans. Unable to proceed barefoot on the scorching streets, they took refuge in a pagoda. The thick walls of the shrine shielded them from the fire. The nuns, who wore tongs, ran on to get help.

Within half an hour, Mother Mary of the Holy Family, the Mother Superior of the Convent, rescued the girls and led them via another route to safety.

At Mandalay Hill to the north-east of the city, the Japanese remained in their warren of underground bunkers. Snipers shot at the Ghurkha troops advancing to the summit. Allied engineers used explosives to burst concrete fortifications; soldiers poured petrol and dropped grenades into cavities.

Meanwhile, the Frontier Force regiment cleared pockets of the enemy still hiding in houses, before attacking Fort Dufferin. Two hundred civilians had been interned at the southern end, but the Japanese drove the prisoners from the air-raid shelters. The inmates raced towards the trees and lay flat on their stomachs, cowering from the bombs.

The fort had brick buttresses ten metres thick at ground level, and three metres at the top. Skip-bombing proved unsuccessful in penetrating these solid walls.

The next morning, planes bombed the fort again, and an advance patrol stormed in. Prisoners ran forward, laughing and cheering at the sight of their rescuers. The officer-in-charge of the platoon handed a Union Jack to one of them and ordered him to climb the flagpole. The young man, Tony Rowsen, tied a white sheet to a bamboo pole and climbed onto the roof, waving the makeshift white flag and the British colours.

Seeing the flags, the pilots withheld their bombs and radioed headquarters, informing them the fort had surrendered.

Fort Dufferin was the last stronghold in Mandalay to fall.

On 20 March 1945, after three weeks of fierce fighting, the Allies declared the city safe for civilians. The war was over for us.

***

We moved into the house Mum had inherited from her parents. I still remember the address—No 26, 24th Street. The building was not far from the fort. Built of solid red brick, it had three bedrooms, a dining room, kitchen and a large lounge room. A bomb had destroyed the walls of the bathroom, but Dad and the boys put up a temporary partition of metal sheets.

The infamous *Kempetai* had occupied the place and left in a hurry, leaving behind a grand piano in the sitting room. It grinned at us like a skull I'd seen at a museum.

Mum's fingers strayed to the keys. 'This can partly compensate for the one we left at Rangoon during the evacuation.'

My thoughts flew back to Mum's piano and all my dolls and toys. I rushed towards the other rooms. In the bedroom, Rupert and Bertie gazed at the dead body of a Japanese officer. I stopped and stared at the corpse.

Mum pulled me back until the boys dragged out the cadaver by its legs. They left it in the gardens of Queen Alexandria's Children's Hospital, behind our house.

Rupert kept the skull on the shelf beside his bed. The cranium displayed a fine set of teeth and gave me a toothy grin. It had a terrible stink, so I tried to stay away from his room until no odour remained. The skull fascinated me, however, and I often returned to gaze at it and wonder where the departed soul now lived.

The Japanese had used the building behind ours as a military hospital and, in the months of fighting around Mandalay, it had filled with casualties. Orderlies had laid their dead in rows, and hundreds of corpses lay awaiting cremation. In the hospital grounds, too, cadavers piled up during the clean-up of Mandalay by Allied forces.

Rupert spent hours following the soldiers and watching them at work. 'How do you defuse a land mine?' he asked a sapper.

'It's simple. Just remove the detonator.' The sapper unscrewed a mine in front of him.

Rupert thanked him and occupied his time deactivating mines and collecting empty shell cases. He gave them to Mum.

She rubbed the brass casings until they shone. Then she used them as vases.

***

As soon as the Allies had cleared the hospital grounds, Rupert searched for more corpses. Rummaging among the reeds in the moat, he discovered bloated bodies of Allied soldiers who'd tried to cross it during the fighting. The treacherous weeds had encircled their arms and legs, embracing them in a watery grave.

At about this time, when the corpses of Japanese soldiers still lay unburied, Rover strayed from home and delved among the bodies. Dogs snarled and fought each other over the fly-blown cadavers. Rover brought us part of a human body. He dropped the foul-smelling flesh and bone at our feet and wagged his tail. We couldn't tolerate the stench and chased him off.

Slinking into the shadows with his bone, he never returned. Perhaps soldiers shot him or he fell ill from consuming rotting human flesh.

We remained inconsolable at his loss. He was our companion in distress, and we couldn't bring ourselves to get another dog until years later.

***

When the army completed their clean-up of the area, Rupert turned his attention to Mandalay Hill where the dead lay strewn all over the hillside. The 19th Indian Division had driven deep into the town. Ghurkhas had been engaged in fierce hand-to-hand combat there.

Rupert climbed the hill, ignoring the path usually taken by pilgrims and visitors. He struggled through the mass of tangled growth, searching for souvenirs.

Later that day, wrapping his trophies in newspaper, he danced home in triumph. Placing the bundle on our table, he produced a Japanese soldier's foot and a curved *kukri* that once belonged to a Ghurkha. I retreated slightly, fascinated by his spoils.

Rupert said, 'Ghurkhas have two *kukris*. One is a dress *kukri*, which he wears on ceremonial occasions, like the parades we used to attend on New Year's Day. He uses the other in battle, and when cleaning or sharpening the blade, he has to draw blood before putting it away. If no enemy is in sight, he deliberately cuts himself.'

The Japanese soldier's foot was a gruesome object. Yellow toe nails were still embedded in the bony sockets of the withered appendage. Rupert pulled its tendons and made it walk towards me. I screamed.

Mum came to the rescue and fell into a fit of laughing. It occurred to me I had not heard her laugh for a long time.

The foot and the *kukri* joined the skull on the shelves beside Rupert's bed. His room smelled horribly, but I'd sometimes steal in to gaze at the dried tissue and muscles, and marvel at the number of little bones in a person's foot.

In spite of his attraction for war trophies, my brother had a tender side. He took Rose for rides on his cycle. On one occasion, making a complete circuit of the moat, he discovered some tomato plants with ripe juicy fruit.

Rose picked as many tomatoes as she could. The outing seemed a wonderful adventure to her and both had such a good time they arrived home late.

We had fresh tomatoes in our salad that evening. Perhaps the tomatoes saved Rupert from a whipping.

Bertie entertained the family, singing all the latest songs like *Dear Hearts and Gentle People*, *Music, Music, Music*, *I'd have Baked a Cake*, and *Good Night Irene*.

Rose joined in with *Rudolf the Red-Nosed Reindeer*, and *How much is that Doggie in the Window?* She loved to sing, and filled our home with song and laughter. She wandered from room to room, lost in wonder. She'd never lived in such a big house.

I imagined the happiness awaiting us when we returned to Rangoon. Still, in May 1945, the fighting was far from over. It continued for another three months over the southern hills and the Sittang River towards Thailand.

Chapter 23

Victory

Early in July, Mr Barry visited Dad. He looked lean and sun-tanned.

'Where've you been?' Dad asked.

'Lying low during the fighting.' Barry winked. 'We should be back in Rangoon shortly.' He gave the victory sign. 'Things will soon return to normal.'

'I hope so.' Dad broke into a smile.

Barry shook his head. 'The war's not over yet and reconstruction will take years.'

I pressed my lips flat and held my arms close to my body. I'd hoped everything would be just as before.

After an uncomfortable pause, Barry continued, 'Old D'Cruz died during the trek to India.'

D'Cruz had been Dad's immediate superior. I'd often overheard him say, *'The man lords it over me.'*

He sat up straight and failed to hide his delight. 'His wife must be happy. He gave her a hard time.'

Barry winked. 'Yes, but she had a good shoulder to cry upon.'

'With little enough comfort at home, she needed someone to talk to.'

Barry cleared his throat. 'We knew about your meetings with Mrs D'Cruz. Visiting her whenever the old man was on tour at the district courts.'

'Well?'

'But you didn't let your private life interfere with work.'

Dad's face clouded.

'Don't worry. Don't worry.' Barry laughed, putting up both hands to ward off an imaginary blow. 'I won't say a word to your wife.'

The staff at the High Court seemed to know everything, and Dad had obviously forgotten servants couldn't keep their mouths shut. Barry rose to leave. 'I must get back as soon as possible and secure good living quarters for my family.'

***

After the fall of Mandalay, Allied forces overwhelmed the Japanese garrison at Maymyo. They cut the rail link between Japanese troops in central and northern Burma. In April, they accepted the surrender of Chandra Bose's Indian National Army, which had been fighting for the Japanese.

On reading the news, Mum reached out and squeezed my hand. Then she released her hold and made the sign of the cross. I let my head fall against her and shut my eyes.

The next few months were happy and peaceful. Dad still drank at nights, but he didn't quarrel with Mum or belt any of us. He repaired the house and put putty on the gaping shrapnel holes in the roof.

The enemy had attempted to destroy some electric fans. They'd thrown them down a well in the hospital yard behind our place. Rupert and Bertie retrieved them with a rope and a hook and Dad checked whether they were still in working order. He then put an advertisement in the local newspaper.

The next morning, people knocked at our door, and kept streaming in even after the fans had gone.

Someone offered to buy the piano, so Dad sold it. 'Now we have sufficient money for food to tide us over until I return to work.'

Unable to bear the sight of the men bearing away our piano, I covered my face with my hands. Mum placed her hand on my shoulder. 'We can't take it with us to Rangoon, and we need cash for essential items.'

I bit my lip. *How could I tell Mum that I wanted everything to be as it had been before?*

***

Dad bought the papers every day. We learned that, while the Allies fought in the suburbs of Mandalay, the 17th Indian army attacked Meiktila, a Japanese garrison less than a hundred and fifty kilometres south. When the town fell, over two thousand Japanese corpses lay in bunkers and cellars; bloated bodies floated on the lake.

On hearing the news, warmth radiated through me. I swaggered about the house, a smile on my lips. Young as I was, I couldn't help gloating over the crushing victory.

Prior to the conquest of Burma, Aung San and his Thirty Comrades aided invading Japanese troops. They promised freedom for Burma, but within a few years Aung San was disillusioned. On 27 March 1945, the Burma National Army—now the Patriot Burmese Forces—broke out in rebellion against the Japanese.

Undercover agents promised Aung San safe conduct to British Headquarters, and Lieutenant-Colonel Bartells, then a captain, escorted him to meet General Slim on 16 May.

Years later, the Lieutenant-Colonel gave me details of the meeting. Aung San wore the uniform of a Japanese general. General Slim sported a Ghurkha hat and unkempt trousers. Seeing Aung San in the uniform of a Japanese general, Slim's face grew grim. He rebuked him for surrendering only because the Allies were winning the war.

'What would have been the point otherwise?' Aung San replied.

***

Lieutenant General Honda, the Japanese commander of the 33rd Army, retreated southwards to the hills of the Pegu Yomas. There his men had set up dumps of food and ammunition. They dug in, living on rice, bamboo shoots, grass and lizards. Day after day, many attempted to break out and make a run for Thailand. The desertions only stopped when the men became too weak for further attempts.

The Burmese army had changed sides by then. They stalked the Japanese and wreaked vengeance upon their former allies.

Barely six thousand of eighteen thousand Japanese reached the eastern bank of the Sittang River, where Allied Forces had suffered disaster in

1942. The Allies shot down any of the enemy attempting to cross on rafts or logs. The strong currents swept away corpses and survivors alike. Others died through lack of food and medical supplies.

Malaria and typhus added to the toll but, unable to accept defeat, the Japanese chose to collapse and die where they fought.

***

When the 14th Army advanced into Burma from India, skeletons lay propped against trees. The remains of men, women and children shrouded in rags, and soldiers from the trek in 1942, were huddled together. Sometimes bamboo had grown through the skeletons and raised them towards heaven as if on an altar. At the oil fields of Yenangaung, the scene of heavy fighting in 1942, the soldiers vindicated their fallen comrades and shelled the enemy until they were annihilated.

Early in 1945, Allied planes bombed the railways. Japanese troops dragged a thousand veterans of the Thai–Burma railway from hospitals and forced-marched them through dense jungle to build a road into Thailand.

After Rangoon fell, Japanese troops attempted to escape via this new road.

***

Since the spring of 1945, formations of Allied bombers, escorted by Spitfires and Hurricanes, had bombed Rangoon. Whole city blocks were razed to the ground, the electrical power station was reduced to rubble, the sewer system in a state of collapse, the water supply cut off and the harbour destroyed.

Without its vital organs, the burned-out city was in its death throes. The Japanese commander fled from Rangoon, taking four hundred able-bodied prisoners-of-war as coolies.

Three days after the enemy departed, Allied amphibious assault craft landed at the port on 2 May. Everything of value was destroyed. Filth, over half a metre high, lay in the streets. Power had to be restored and sewerage works reconstructed.

Soon Rangoon filled with squatters and refugees who lived in makeshift huts or crammed into abandoned houses.

***

The government built a breakwater of order amid the raging sea of a war-torn capital. Allied forces were still mopping up Japanese soldiers holding out in the jungles when Dad received a letter from the High Court at Rangoon, advising him to report for work. The government offered him a senior position and enclosed a cheque. As accommodation was scarce in post-war Rangoon, they requested him not to take us with him.

Wide grins spread over our faces and our eyes sparkled when he left. We were free. Free to have friends and free to enjoy life. Our time without Dad had a profound effect upon me. Mum used the few drops of eau de cologne she had hoarded during the war. The perfume lingered on in some subterranean cavern of my senses and I always associate that fragrance with her. A mantle of peace descended.

We received weekly rations because Dad was once more an employee of the British government. Before his departure, he authorised Rupert to collect the coupons from the army canteen on his behalf. Each week, the boys brought home tins of bully beef, sausages—and tickets to the Garrison Theatre.

Every weekend, British soldiers provided a concert featuring talented musicians and singers from their ranks. Sometimes they had a film. On Saturday evenings, Rupert and Bertie took me with them, while Mum stayed at home with Herman and Rose. The bombing had destroyed most of Mandalay, and in places only building facades remained. The theatre was nothing more than a Nissan hut. At the first concert a soldier sang *You are my Sunshine*. I forgot my surroundings, our past sufferings and the war. Thrills of excitement rippled down my spine and my pulse raced. Bertie obtained the words and in no time we were singing it too. I vividly recall the cartoon and song that went: *The red, red robin goes bob-bob-bobbing along*. How wonderful life was!

In December, the Red Cross held a Christmas party for children. Memories of December 1941 came flooding back: Mum planning to send me with June to meet Santa but, instead of presents, Japanese bombs had rained down.

How different it was now. Instead of being the younger sister, I was the elder. As we queued to receive gifts from Santa, I gripped my sister's hand and saw the wonder sparkling in her eyes. Our *first* party.

Rose ran up to Father Christmas and received a little Red Riding Hood rag doll. I hung back, even though I longed for a doll. I thought of the Christmas party June and I were to attend years before. I smoothed my dress, then stepped aside for the girl behind me to move forward. I couldn't go up to receive a gift without June.

***

On June 14, representatives of all units and organisations participating in the Burma Campaign joined the Victory Parade in Rangoon. Amid the ringing of church bells, a Lancaster bomber dropped one million poppies like droplets of blood.

Two months later, when the first atomic bomb plummeted down on Japan, followed by another, three days later, World War II finally ended.

The Burma campaign had lasted thirty-two months.

***

When we heard the news, Mum shed tears of joy. She hugged Rose and waltzed around the room. Rupert's eyes danced. He kept fisting his open palm with his right fist. Bertie whistled *Rule Britannia*.

A feeling of weightlessness swept over me. I imagined myself flying on a magic carpet, looking down at the town below as we headed towards Rangoon.

Chapter 24

A Period of Peace

Soon schools re-opened in Mandalay. Mum enrolled Rose and me at her old school, St. Joseph's Convent, and the boys at St. Peter's, Dad's alma mater. She bought navy blue material and hand-sewed uniforms for the two of us. I was now nearly in my teens but my breasts were no bigger than two buttons.

We had missed four years of schooling, but our teachers taught us an academic year's work in six months and put us up a grade. They held examinations semi-annually and promoted those who passed. Most students were eager to study and we soon caught up with our lost years in the next eighteen months. Some, however, had no interest in education—especially those girls more interested in dating soldiers than studying.

Rose won the hearts of all the nuns. They selected her for the school concert. I sewed her a white dress and, like Shirley Temple, she sang *On the Good Ship Lollipop* and *Animal Crackers in My Soup*. As she sang and danced, we smiled and held our heads high.

Rupert and Bertie had been wearing native *loongyis*, having put aside their western clothes for better day. But they had grown and had to squeeze into those they'd worn during the evacuation from Katha. Mum managed to buy them a shirt each, but they could barely fit into their shorts. It made me realise how much they'd grown.

We were unable to buy any trousers or shorts until shops replenished their supplies of western clothing.

Allied troops used St. Peter's Boys' School as a hospital for sick and wounded soldiers, so the government allowed the Christian Brothers to open their school at Queen Alexandria Children's Hospital behind our house. Rupert and Bertie only had to jump over the fence to enter the grounds.

All traces of corpses, shells, grenades and land-mines had disappeared.

***

The Japanese had promised freedom to Burma, and the people now demanded liberty. The Burmese Nationalist Movement had commenced early in the twentieth century. It had gathered impetus when, in 1929, Gandhi visited Burma, asking Indians to boycott all foreign manufactured cloth.

Burmese activists U Ottama, U Wisara and Aung San had colluded with him and the Indian National Congress to agitate for independence. Like the Gandhi homespun campaign in India, U Ottama, a Buddhist monk, had popularised the wearing of local handmade cloth in Burma.

Burmese nationalists showed their distaste for colonial rule by donning native dress—a *loongyi*, jacket, a cloth headdress and slippers, rather than European suits and shoes.

We had a foretaste of the seething rebellion when one of the Rupert's fellow-students, dissatisfied with his grades, decided to avenge himself on his teacher, Brother Adrian. One day during a Chemistry class, the student crept behind his teacher with a golf club, and struck him. The brother fell forward on his desk but quickly rose and, with blood streaming from his wound, chased his attacker.

Such an incident would have been unheard of in pre-war days.

Britain had always entrusted Anglo-Indians with important jobs but most Burmese referred to us as *half-caste*, a term originating in India when Indian women married outside their caste.

Bertie convinced me people of mixed origin possessed the best qualities of both races. He taught me to be proud of my origins. 'Look at the mule—it's a cross between a horse and a donkey, but it has the strength of the horse, with the sure-footedness of the donkey. We inherit the best traits from both races.'

***

Mandalay had a rural atmosphere and, although the second largest city of Burma, it was much smaller than Rangoon. Since the war had left us impoverished, we had no servant to escort us to school. Sick and lame pariah dogs covered by mange and running sores wandered unchecked on the streets. Some, crippled by arthritis, dragged their useless hind legs, snarling at everyone. Buddhists, with their doctrine of re-incarnation, did not believe in putting down a sick or lame dog, thus magnifying the problem.

In the heat of summer, when rabies was rampant, we walked to school with a stone or stick in our hands to defend ourselves from dogs. My hands turned clammy and the hair on my neck rose whenever news spread of a rabid dog roaming the streets. Each morning, we hurried to school with yelping, howling and snapping pariahs at our heels. At times, we'd see a solitary dog nosing the grass on the kerb, sniffing for scraps of food. The dog would watch us with one paw raised. If it loped towards us, I'd throw a stone to discourage it from following us, and glance back, searching for flecks of foam on the mouth—a tell-tale symptom of rabies.

One summer day, a group of shouting men sprinted up the road behind us. At first, I didn't hear what they were yelling. When they grew closer, the cry, 'Mad dog. Mad dog,' reached me.

A crossbreed, part-mastiff and part bulldog, tore along the road. Its head was down, its hair bristled and foam frothed around its snout.

It was less than fifty metres away. Its tail was down—its mouth open. It came closer—close enough for me to distinguish the yellow-red eyes and open sores on the canine's forelegs. Saliva dribbled on the path.

I grabbed Rose by her hand and dashed into a neighbour's yard, shutting the gate. At that moment, one of the men caught up with the mongrel and threw a net over it. The dog, enmeshed, continued to run. The man hung on until others arrived and attacked it with large blunt weapons.

The dog looked ferocious even in death. Its jaws yawned open, exposing its fangs.

Still trembling, I unlatched the gate and led my sister away. I dreaded the thought of having injections in my stomach to counteract the effect of rabies.

Despite the pariah-dogs and the heat, we were delighted to be alive, and slowly recovered from the effects of malnutrition. Mum revelled in her new-found freedom. She hummed and sang, visited the Convent and met her old teachers. She looked radiant with a vitality I had not seen before. Her steps were firmer, her stance straighter.

The nuns arranged for Mum to meet a priest in the Chapel, where she received the Sacraments for the first time in years.

I found friends. Colleen Soord became very dear to me. Our mothers had known each other at school and Mum allowed me to visit her. I recalled Dad refusing to let me go to my best friend's birthday party so many years before. Now I grasped the cup of joy with both hands.

Colleen's mother had engaged a tutor for her in mathematics and Mum coached me in Algebra, while Bertie untangled the mysterious web surrounding Geometry. With this extra coaching, Colleen and I excelled in maths and were always the first to complete our sums in class.

One day, I took up my work to have it checked. My Maths teacher, Sister D'Chantal, pointed to another desk further off and told me to sit there. She must have thought I'd copied the sums off Colleen, as I shared the same desk with my new friend.

My nails bit into the palms of my hand as I stumbled back to my place and collected my books as she ordered. Then I slid into a seat in the far corner of the room.

The next day, to prove I hadn't cheated, I made sure I was first to take my sums to the nun. Sister D'Chantal marked the work in silence, avoided my eyes and handed back my book.

I walked back triumphant. I had redeemed my name.

Not long after, she allowed us to sit together again.

***

Colleen was my guardian angel. A year older than me, it seemed God had sent her in June's place. Every lunch hour, she took me along when she visited the convent Chapel. She taught me how to use the holy water from the font at the entrance, to genuflect before I entered the pews and explained the meaning of the little box on the altar.

At first I went along to please her, but soon the peace pervading its precincts attracted me. I often slipped in alone to pray.

Once, when spending the day at Colleen's place, she introduced me to Joe, the man Mum had almost married. Tall and handsome, his brown eyes shone with kindness. He held both my hands and gazed at me. 'You have May's eyes.'

That evening, I asked her why we could not continue living as we did now and *never* return to Rangoon.

Mum listened intently. A sigh shook her like a shiver, and she answered in her usual sad way. 'I cannot abandon Herman. Neither will I be able to cope with the burden of taking care of him.'

I sometimes speculated whether my words had affected Mum. Deep down in her the seed of freedom must have germinated, but at the time I wondered if she had forgotten the cruel beatings.

Little did I grasp the consequences for a wife who attempted to leave her husband!

As time passed, I began to understand Mum and came to sense her unspoken words. No social services were available at that time but I hoped we'd someday enjoy the sweet fruits of freedom forever. *When would that happen?* I grew impatient—like a racehorse pawing the ground in a ceaseless endeavour to commence the race.

For years, it had required an extraordinary effort to survive. Now Mum constantly wore a smile. The boys constructed a transistor in their science class, and it proved a good substitute for our pre-war radio.

Mum taught me how to waltz when suitable music played. She was affectionate in her touch, stroking our arms and shoulders, without having to hold back her emotions. Bertie was particularly happy, as Dad had never allowed him to embrace Mum.

Years later, Bertie told me how frustrated he'd been on seeing his cousin, Henry, place his arms around his mother, Aunt Jhan, while he, a non-Muslim, was denied the right to hug his own mother.

***

With the war over and the steady flow of cash from Dad, money seemed a small problem. It became easy to forget the hardships we endured.

While Dad was in Rangoon, we lived in happiness and peace. I now no longer desired to go home. Mum often tilted back her head and sat with her eyes closed and a satisfied smile upon her face. We all had an unflagging zest for life; our laughter flowed like a rippling brook.

War had brought everyone closer. Those who survived cherished life so much more. Mum visited her old friends, chatted of past times, and caught up with news of their growing families.

People re-built war-torn buildings. Merchandise soon spilled out of shop fronts and we could buy almost anything we wanted. Mum bought shorts for the boys and dress material for Rose and me. As the weeks passed, normality edged back.

***

One September night in 1946, I awoke, sure that a great hand was shaking my bed. I sprang to my feet, thinking bombs were dropping again.

'Earthquake. Earthquake,' Mum screamed. 'Run outside and sit on the ground.' Her hair was in disarray, and she had a harried look on her face.

I rushed towards the lawn in front of our house. Mum led Rose, while Bertie carried Herman. Rupert saw that everyone was safe—then stumbled out as the next tremor tumbled vases and crockery from the shelves.

The ground moved in waves beneath me. A snail drew time's chariot and eternity stood still. I wanted to get up and run, but remained glued to the spot. I imagined the force of the tremor would fling me down if I rose. I expected cracks and caverns to yawn open in the ground. I wondered if the house, peppered with bullet holes and shrapnel, and weakened by the vibration of bombs, would withstand the shaking.

The old building swayed on its foundations and pieces of plaster fell from the wall, filling the air with dust. However, it acquired only a few new cracks in its walls.

Further down the road, part of a Buddhist monastery collapsed, burying a monk beneath the debris. The boys raced over to witness the damage. It looked just like another war-torn building. A monk had died and several others were injured.

***

A year sped past. My parents corresponded regularly. One day when the postman delivered mail, Mum opened a letter and, with an Arctic smile, handed it to me.

Without reading, I guessed what it contained. 'Come immediately,' Dad wrote. 'We've been granted government quarters.'

The white quarto-sized paper dispelled all my dreams. I shuddered at the thought of forfeiting our freedom. Many times I'd pleaded with Mum not to join Dad in Rangoon, but to no avail. She insisted people would treat her as an outcast. No social services meant no money. How could women survive in a man's world?

I longed to disentangle myself from the net closing around us. For years, I'd looked forward to Rangoon, but now the prospect chilled me. What were riches compared to freedom?

Yet if the master calls, the slave must obey. Mum prepared for the trip to Rangoon. She would no longer be permitted to visit the nuns or receive the Sacraments. She'd no longer see our faces light up with joy.

For nearly two years, we'd lived a normal life despite the reminders of war all around. I'd come to savour the sweetness of peace, along with a subdued animosity against my father. However, as the letter's message burnt into my soul, all dislike for him flooded back. It leapt out of the shadows, reminding me of our sufferings. The turmoil of war seemed nothing in comparison to life with him.

I shivered. Like a draught of icy air, the letter set me coughing. With drooping shoulders, I helped Mum pack, realising she was powerless to act against his wishes.

Her silent acceptance was worse than tears.

The past months had been one long vacation which would never return. The thought of relinquishing our freedom filled me with despair. A butterfly with newly acquired wings caught in a web, my struggles secured me tighter and tighter until my delicate wings were torn and useless. I could not fly away.

***

Mum packed her portmanteau, a wooden box and our household goods—then left us to complete packing our cases. She went to say goodbye to the nuns and all her old friends. On her return, she choked as she asked Rupert and Bertie to arrange train tickets for the trip. When they left, she spoke with tears in her eyes. 'I walked along the streets of Mandalay for the last time, pondering on what the future would bring.' Dabbing her eyes with her handkerchief, she handed me a neat brown parcel. 'Your birthday's coming up soon. I want you to have your present before we leave.'

The weight, the sharp corners and the hard surface told me the package contained a book. In feverish haste, I opened the parcel. *Good Wives*.

I kissed her lightly on her cheek. 'Thank you, Mum.'

'When I wrote to your father and told him what I'd bought you, he said it'll put ideas into your head. Read the book and hide it away from him. He doesn't want me to give it to you, but you loved reading *Little Women*, so I thought you'd like to have the sequel.' She hung her head and compressed her lips.

I put my arms around her, holding her close. 'I'd love to know what happens to Jo.' *It's one thing to dream of a Prince Charming, but with Mum's unhappy marriage before me, how could I ever consider marrying?*

Chapter 25

Sustained by Hope

In a daze, we stood on the station platform while the boys went off to locate our seats. They returned, waving the tickets above their heads and chatting to each other.

'We can get on now.' Rupert chose a comfortable corner in a second-class carriage.

They appeared happy, but I saw through their poor attempt at cheer and guessed that they, too, were not happy to re-join Dad. They were young men now, and I was sure they didn't relish the thought of having their freedom curtailed. Placing my feet on a suitcase, I sat brooding by the window, my head cupped in my hands. The case contained the bundle of frocks Dad's relatives had given us during the war. Beautifully tailored dresses left by refugees trekking across the Himalayas to India. I'd been too small then, but now with a few alterations they fitted me.

As the train rattled towards Rangoon, the fun and frolic of the past eighteen months vanished. Torn from a peaceful harbour, I tossed on the ocean of sorrow. A weight seemed to press down upon me.

A speck of coal dust blew in, bringing tears to my eyes.

'Are you all right, Hazel?' Mum asked.

I nodded, trying not to compound her worry.

She stroked my hand. 'I've something to tell you. Your father offered you in marriage to Henry.'

'What!' I withdrew my hand from Mum's touch. 'I'm too young to marry and will *never* consent to an arranged marriage.'

She tilted her head to one side. 'If he forces you?'

'I'll run away. Anywhere.' I folded my arms.

'Fortunately, your uncle is a devout Muslim. He rejected the offer, saying you're a non-believer and unworthy of his son, a good Muslim.'

I sighed with relief. I considered myself a freethinker, free to think as I chose, even if restrained in all else. I wanted to be like other girls—to meet friends of both sexes and attend parties. What did life hold out for me? I'd reached my teens, but had nothing to look forward to.

Henry was my favourite cousin—a friend and childhood playmate—but the thought of marrying him repulsed me. I abhorred arranged marriages, so common in Muslim families. Besides, I did not want to marry so young.

My eyes dimmed as I churned over Mum's situation. *How could she live like this? Why did she accept such wretchedness and not fight back? Surely, death was preferable to abject misery.* I tried to visualise my future, but sickening fear smothered me. The train rattled on. I recalled our journey from Katha to Mandalay when the Japanese had taken the whole of Burma. June had been with me then.

I gazed out of the window. Bombed-out railway stations, incinerated engines and carriages riddled with machine-gun bullets lay rusting where they had fallen. The earth, ashamed of the disfigurement, covered itself with grass. Saplings and vines grew over the wagons in a desperate attempt to hide the scars of war. The burned-out skeleton of a tree waved at us, a reminder of its former glory.

We passed a bullock-cart filled with hay. The bulls shook their heads in a futile effort to shake the flies off their noses. My eyes fastened on the beasts until they were no more than a speck on the horizon.

The train snorted its way across the plains towards Rangoon, belching out billows of smoke and causing me to withdraw from the window, unable to shake off the profound sadness weighing me down. My brothers had some freedom but, as a girl, I had nothing before me. I turned heavenwards for help.

The stars were covered by a wild flight of clouds. Like them, we were leaving behind a jewelled sky and hurrying towards darkness.

Throughout the war, I'd dreamed of my dolls and the happy, carefree times with June. I'd longed for Rangoon. Now, with a haunting sense of foreboding, I only wanted freedom.

Swept away on the infinite river of time, grey and drizzly dawns spread before my mind's eye. I knew happiness would vanish in the gloom of Rangoon; the wonderful times we had together so recently would soon disintegrate to nothing but a memory.

The occasional breath of wind told me the weather was about to change. A slight breeze blew in, making me shiver. The terrors of the past rose before me once again.

I fell asleep, waking from time to time as we steamed through the night—one thought uppermost in my mind. *Will we never succeed in breaking the bonds binding us to our jailer?*

***

All our chatter and joy vanished when, on a sweltering day in April, the train hissed to a halt like the serpent of Paradise. The scar incised on my memory remains forever. Dad waited on the platform. He stood a couple of metres back from the carriage, his hands on his hips and a frown on his face. The heat shimmering up from the concrete floor shrouded him in a hot, humid blanket.

With a more mature appreciation of my father's true nature, I realise an impregnable wall had arisen, dividing us. My heart at its lowest ebb, I gazed at his lean frame and sullen face. He seemed sterner than ever. Perhaps he resented the freedom we had enjoyed and sensed our unhappiness at reuniting with him.

An uncomfortable silence followed. Slowly, Mum stepped down from the carriage, walked over to him, and stood before him—stiff and erect. His lips brushed her cheek. After eighteen months of separation, my parents greeted each other with affected affection! Not at all like Prince Charming in *The Sleeping Beauty* who awoke his princess with a fervent kiss.

I knew their love no longer existed.

Rupert and Bertie descended, carrying our cases. Filled with apprehension, I stepped from the carriage. Our father must have noticed we had put on weight. I think he realised we had grown estranged from him.

Rose was the last to leave the carriage. Once on the platform, she stopped and peered at him shyly.

He opened his arms. She ran towards him and returned his kiss.

He grunted a greeting to Rupert and barely acknowledged Bertie and me.

Once the boys had loaded our luggage on a gharry, my father gave directions to the Supreme Court. I wondered why he was going to his workplace and not taking us to our quarters. As we drove along the now unfamiliar streets, the derelict structures around us were in concord with my own gloomy thoughts. Plaster and paint were peeling off the buildings. Badly in need of repair, they spoke of past grandeur and years of neglect. Residents had dragged away burned timber beams for firewood. Piles of twisted metal, masonry and bricks were all that remained of many grand houses, fine shops and thriving factories.

Some instinctive sense sent a series of warning signals through the corridors of my mind. The black raven of fear, sitting on my shoulder, flapped its wings as we drove towards what was to be our home.

***

On our arrival at the Supreme Court, our father informed us the government had allocated us a storeroom in the grounds as living quarters. He led us in silence. The large padlock hanging on a rusty chain grated when he turned the key. A gush of cold musty air greeted us as he flung open the door, bringing to mind the damp trench in which we had sheltered from the bombs. Goose pimples broke out all over as I peered into the dark interior. I rubbed my arms to keep them warm.

Dad fumbled with the light switch. The click echoed back at us, illuminating a bare concrete floor devoid of beds or furniture except for one unpolished wooden chair and table.

'Our box and cases can serve as chairs. The toilets and bathroom are in another part of the building. This will be our home until better accommodation is available.' In the void, his voice echoed our doom.

The storeroom had only one window with iron bars, like a prison. I'd expected to return to the comfortable government quarters we'd lived in before the war. I glanced at Mum. Her face was expressionless, her eyes glazed. We had brought along a few bamboo mats rolled up and tied with a string. She cut the string, unrolled the mats and tossed our bedding on them.

The dreary room was horrible—even more reprehensible than the village huts. How I despised my father for deceiving us! *Had his relatives at Mandalay spied on us, and reported on the freedom we'd been enjoying?*

Next morning, we peered through the windows and watched the judges and solicitors arrive in their shiny cars. Fully decked out in their wigs and cowls, they walked past on the balconies.

We had to keep quiet during office hours and particularly when the court was in session. The storeroom was only a few metres off the main building. Herman, who was prone to bouts of loud crying, posed quite a problem. However no obstacle was insurmountable to my father. He instructed Bertie to carry Herman to one of the side gates each morning, place him in a chair and leave him there to amuse himself, watching passers-by on the road.

Every day, Herman sat in the shade—out of sight and hearing of the judges. He made feeble attempts at clapping when happy, and tried to tear people's hair out if they came within arm's reach.

One morning, a young Burmese girl used the gardens as a short cut to her work. Herman clapped his hands as she passed. His teeth turned and crossed at awkward angles—and his breath stank. His tongue hung out, saliva streaming from his mouth.

The girl, thinking he was making a pass at her, spat out a string of abuse. 'I'll slap you with this on your impertinent face.' She took off her slipper.

Herman continued drooling.

She stepped forward, her eyes blazing, hand poised above his head.

Just then, I came along with a glass of water for my brother and, sizing up the situation, pleaded with her to understand he was a victim of infantile paralysis and not responsible for his actions.

Mollified by my explanation and apologies, the girl dropped her weapon, slipped her foot into it and proceeded on her way.

Although relieved I'd saved saved Herman from a beating, I wanted to run away and hide. My knees however were locked together. To acknowledge that this idiot who sat at the gate was my brother had been the ultimate humiliation. Shame overwhelmed me, and I wished to disown him. I'd loved him as an infant when he looked like any other baby. Yet as time passed he neither talked nor walked and grew more repulsive, especially after he lost his milk teeth.

Mum regarded Herman as a punishment sent to her from God for marrying out of her church. During the war, she had once pointed out the village idiot and told us he was the son of a priest who had gone astray, forsaken his vows, and lived with a native woman. 'It's God's punishment,' she said sorrowfully.

***

The Supreme Court janitor and his family stayed upstairs at the opposite end of the building with proper facilities but we lived in cramped conditions with no kitchen or toilet.

We had bread with butter and jam for breakfast, sandwiches for lunch. Dad bought some takeaway food for dinner. The toilet was within walking distance, but we were only allowed to shower before the court sessions commenced, or after they ended in the evening. Water had always been in short supply during the war. Now I delighted in feeling it caress my body as I stood beneath the shower and lathered myself with sweet-scented soap. The only pleasure I had while we lived in the storeroom.

In the evenings, when the judges departed, Bertie carried Herman back in. Yet, after dinner, our father drove us out. 'Get some fresh air. Sit under the balcony of the court house and have a sing-along.' He made it seem as though we were illicit dwellers.

I couldn't understand his sudden love of music. I recalled the time he slapped my face when I sang in the futile hope of bringing June back to earth.

'Don't ever let me hear you singing again,' he had said, while his slap rang in my ears. Yet now he ordered us to sing.

The boys looked knowingly at each other. They headed to the place Dad had indicated, while Rose and I followed.

They sank down on the marble steps, and Bertie commenced singing. Rose sat beside him, clapping her hands in time to the music, and singing with a clear, bell-like voice.

Dad opened the window and shouted. 'Go on. Everybody sing. Sing louder.'

Rupert then sang, but without enthusiasm. I sang feebly, unable to forget Dad's slap.

***

Mum came out later, and I joined her in front of the cold dwelling. We strolled beneath a canopy of stars in the soft summer breeze. We walked up and down, always within my father's view, while he reclined in our only chair, sipping his grog in the dingy room.

The queen-of-the-night was in full bloom, and its perfume enveloped us in a sense of euphoria. Mum spoke to me of lovers walking hand-in-hand on moonlit nights. Those she had loved and lost lived on in her memories. Old times crowded back on her as she related her stories, filling me with dreams of future freedom. Her flow of eloquence kept me enthralled.

I was conscious of the restless beat of my heart as I listened to Mum's stories. I'd have to wait until legally of age to do as I pleased, unless a knight in shining armour came along and carried me off on his horse.

We walked and talked as the queen-of-the-night spilled out its scent and the murmur of traffic reached us. *Maybe, if ever things became intolerable, I could escape and run off somewhere—but how?*

During my first decade, I'd come to realise life was fragile and happiness transient. I'd suffered fear and pain, and witnessed unspeakable things—but I also learned that hope could not be quenched. My limbs tingled and I licked my lips in thoughtful expectation. I envisaged a bright and wonderful future for myself and I was determined to attain it. Sustained by hope, I fantasised that I would someday find love and liberty. The only question was when.

Gazing at the moonlight on the starry flowers of the queen-of-the night, I knew that I would escape from my father's clutches and be free one day. Free to live a life unfettered by chains.

Acknowledgments

Heaven Tempers the Wind is a work of non-fiction, based on my own experience during World War II, intensive research and interviews held. In some cases, I have disguised the names of certain people to protect their privacy, but names of well-known personalities remain unchanged.

I would like to thank Phillipa Gordon who read and criticised my manuscript at its embryonic stage and encouraged me to proceed with it. I would also like to thank my Writers' Groups, and in particular, Laurie Gilbert, who read the entire manuscript and offered me so much help and encouragement.

My grateful thanks go to Lionel D'Castro, who related to me in vivid detail his encounters on the trek to India; to Johnno, who described the horrifying experience of an ex-Chindit, and all my friends who drew upon their plentiful store of painful memories relating to Burma under Japanese occupation especially Lieutenant Colonel Bartells, who shared with me his memories of the second Arakan invasion and revealed his part in escorting Aung San to meet General Slim soon after the fall of Rangoon when he was a young lieutenant in the armoured tank division.

I am deeply indebted to my husband, Colin, who read my drafts, and was my severest critic. Without his patience and loving support, this book would have been an impossible task.

My very especial gratitude goes to my family for reminding me of incidents we experienced in our childhood and our youth, which had lain hidden in the recesses of my memory, and for important dates I had forgotten.

www.ingramcontent.com/pod-product-compliance
Lightning Source LLC
Chambersburg PA
CBHW030614110526
44587CB00049B/307